Trish Stott

Highly Recommended 1
Workbook Pre-intermediate

English for the hotel and catering industry

OXFORD
UNIVERSITY PRESS

OXFORD

UNIVERSITY PRESS

Great Clarendon Street, Oxford OX2 6DP

Oxford University Press is a department of the University of Oxford.
It furthers the University's objective of excellence in research, scholarship,
and education by publishing worldwide in

Oxford New York

Auckland Cape Town Dar es Salaam Hong Kong Karachi
Kuala Lumpur Madrid Melbourne Mexico City Nairobi
New Delhi Shanghai Taipei Toronto

With offices in

Argentina Austria Brazil Chile Czech Republic France Greece
Guatemala Hungary Italy Japan Poland Portugal Singapore
South Korea Switzerland Thailand Turkey Ukraine Vietnam

OXFORD and OXFORD ENGLISH are registered trade marks of
Oxford University Press in the UK and in certain other countries

ISBN: 978 0 19 457465 5

Printed in China

ACKNOWLEDGEMENTS

Illustrations by: Kathy Baxendale pp 15, 22, 25, 53; Emma Dodd pp 5, 43, 50;
Mark Duffin pp 6, 7, 8, 17, 19, 20, 26, 28, 29, 34, 44, 46, 51; Harry Venning
pp 12, 30, 36, 40, 48

Cover image: Ken Seet/Corbis Flame collection

*The author and publisher are grateful to those who have given permission to reproduce
the following photographs*: Alamy pp 4 (image100), 9 (World Religions Photo
Library); Anthony Blake Picture Library pp 18, 22, 24; Getty Images pp 10
(P.Avis), 14 (B.van der Meer), 15 (Photodisc Red), 16 (Photodisc Green), 32
(G. & M.D.De Lossy), 33 (R.Burke), 36 (P.Seaward), 44 (V C L /C.Ryan),
56 (D.Robb)

Contents

1 Use the clues to find the missing word.

1 P
2 D
3 M
4 C
5 P
6 R
7 K
8 C
9 C
10 R
11 N

1 You reserve this for your car. (7,5)
2 A room for two people. (6,4)
3 There isn't an answer. Take a .... (7)
4 You can see check-in information here. (8,6)
5 It makes paper copies of information from your computer. (7)
6 Another verb for *book*. (7)
7 You key in information on this. (8)
8 Receptionists .... phone callers with rooms. (7)
9 People often pay by .... (6,4)
10 Hotel guests arrive here. (9)
11 *Mr Schmidt's room* .... *is 502.* (6)

2 Use each verb once to complete the sentences.

speak	book	reserve
connect	have	tell
help	make	take

1 Good morning.
   How can I ....*help*....... you?
2 Could I .... a parking
   space for tomorrow?
3 I'd like to .... to
   Roberto Raul, please.
4 One moment,
   I'll .... you.
5 Can I .... a message?
6 I'd like to ....
   a reservation.
7 Please .... her to
   call Valerie.
8 I'd like to .... a room
   for tomorrow night.
9 Can I .... your
   name, please?

3 Underline the correct form.

1 *Can I* / *I'd like* take a message?
2 *Could I* / *I'd like* have your name?
3 *Could I* / *I'd like* to make a
   room reservation.
4 *Could I* / *I'd like* reserve a double
   room for tomorrow night?
5 *Can I* / *I'd like* help you?
6 *Can I* / *I'd like* a cup of coffee.
7 *Could I* / *I'd like* reserve
   a parking space?
8 *Could I* / *I'd like* to book a room
   for tonight.
9 *Can I* / *I'd like* a double room.
10 *Could I* / *I'd like* speak to the
   manager, please?

4 Match sentences 1–8 with responses a–h.

1 | c | Can I have your name, please?
2 | | Could I speak to the manager?
3 | | I'd like to make a reservation for tomorrow.
4 | | I'd like to speak to Mrs Ponti in 342.
5 | | Can I take a message?
6 | | Could I have your number?
7 | | Could I reserve a parking space?
8 | | I'd like to book a double room for tonight.

a Yes. It's 01 274 33 78 91.
b 342. One moment. I'll connect you.
c Ikeda. Mrs Aya Ikeda.
d A parking space for tonight. Yes, sir.
e I'm sorry the manager is in a meeting.
f A double for tonight. Certainly.
g Please tell him to call Dr Graaf.
h Of course. Can I have your name?

---

5 Write the correct greeting or farewell that the reception staff in the pictures are saying.

Mrs Obeda   Dr Obeda   Miss Obeda

2 ....

5 ....

3 ....

6 ....

1 *Good morning, Miss Obeda.*

4 ....

7 ....

2 Giving information

1 Use one word from the box to make hotel and restaurant facilities.

bar	menu	desk	TV
room	facilities	bureau	*park*
cuisine	access	pool	conditioning

car .... *park*

Internet ....

international ....

cocktail ....

à la carte ....

disabled ....

exchange ....

air- ....

swimming ....

satellite ....

information ....

cloak..

---

2 Look at the picture and read the hotel information.
Then underline true or false in sentences 1–8.

HOTEL FELIZ

The Hotel Feliz has 50 bedrooms with air-conditioning, Internet access, and satellite TV. The 40-seat restaurant serves international cuisine. The rooftop swimming pool opens in summer. Shops and exchange bureau in the hotel lobby. Disabled facilities throughout the hotel.

1 There are 150 bedrooms on five floors.	true/*false*
2 There's air-conditioning in the hotel.	true/false
3 There's Internet access in all the bedrooms.	true/false
4 There isn't satellite TV in the rooms.	true/false
5 There are 40 seats in the restaurant.	true/false
6 There aren't any shops in the hotel lobby.	true/false
7 There's an exchange bureau.	true/false
8 There isn't a swimming pool.	true/false

---

3 Use *Is there?/Are there?*, *There is/There are* to complete the dialogue about the Hotel Feliz.

WOMAN: Hello, I'd like some information. ......*Are there*......¹ any disabled facilities in the hotel?

RECEPTIONIST: Yes, ...². We have rooms with disabled facilities and ....³ disabled facilities in the bar and restaurant too.

WOMAN: Good. ....⁴ a car park?

RECEPTIONIST: Yes, ...⁵ a large car park. Guests can reserve a parking space over the phone.

WOMAN: Right. ....⁶ a swimming pool?

RECEPTIONIST: Yes, ...⁷ .

WOMAN: And ....⁸ disabled facilities in the pool?

RECEPTIONIST: Yes, ...⁹ .

WOMAN: That's fine. I'd like to book a room if that's OK.

4 Match phrases 1–10 with facilities a–j.

In a hotel, where would you … ?

1 [e] have a meal   a the swimming pool
2 [   ] change money   b the shops
3 [   ] go for a swim   c the bedroom
4 [   ] buy gifts   d the cloakroom
5 [   ] ask for information   e the restaurant
6 [   ] have a drink   f the laundry
7 [   ] send your dirty clothes g the exchange bureau
8 [   ] park your car   h the information desk
9 [   ] sleep   i the bar
10 [   ] use the toilet   j the car park

5 Correct the mistakes in italics in the text about a restaurant.

EATING OUT

The restaurant is *in* .... *at* ....[1] the top of a tower *at* ....[2] Hong Kong. The tower *has* ....[3] 250 metres high. *They* ....[4] are 150 seats in the restaurant. There *are* ....[5] also a cocktail *café* ....[6]. The restaurant has an à la carte *card* ....[7] and serves international *kitchen* ....[8]. There *is* ....[9] ten waiters and waitresses. There is a *parking* ....[10] at the bottom of the tower.

6 Match the numbers in the pictures with the words.

three hundred   *300* ....   twenty   ....   seventeen   ....
thirty   ....   fifteen   ....   seventy   ....
thirteen   ....   fifty   ....   sixteen   ....
fourteen   ....   eighty   ....   sixty   ....
forty   ....   eighteen ....   ninety   ....
twelve   ....   two hundred .... nineteen   ....

3 Taking room reservations

1 Underline the odd one out.

1 Monday   Tuesday   *tomorrow*   Saturday

2 single   sauna   twin   suite

3 guest   husband   daughter   wife

4 breakfast   departure   lunch   dinner

5 air-conditioning   car park   restaurant   reservation

6 Sunday   September   Wednesday   Friday

7 morning   afternoon   tonight   evening

8 voicemail   email   telephone   arrive

2 Complete the questions and answers with *do/does, don't/doesn't.*

1 ....*Do*....... you have a single room?
   Yes. We ......*do*...... .

2 .... you have a mobile phone number?
   No. I ....

3 .... the hotel have a sauna?
   No. It ....

4 .... the bar open at lunchtime?
   Yes. It ....

5 .... they want adjoining rooms?
   No. They ....

6 .... you have a double room for tonight?
   Yes. We ....

3 Make questions with *Do/Does* using the information in the pictures.

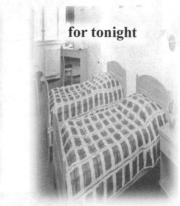

for tonight

1 *Does the hotel have a restaurant?*

3 ....

5 ....

7 ....

Saturday night

2 ....

4 ....

6 ....

8 ....

4 Complete the hotel information with *at, on, in, from … to*.

HOTEL FELIZ
Information for our guests

- Breakfast is served ....._from_.....¹ 7.30 ....² 10.00 in the restaurant.
- The restaurant is open ....³ lunchtime ....⁴ 12.00 ....⁵ 3.00.
- ....⁶ the evening, the restaurant is open ....⁷ 6.00. Last orders are ....⁸ 10.00.
- ....⁹ summer, the terrace restaurant is open ....¹⁰ the evenings.

- The shops in the hotel lobby are open ....¹¹ weekends but the exchange bureau is closed ....¹² Saturday.
- ....¹³ July and August, the swimming pool is open ....¹⁴ 8.00 ....¹⁵ 20.00.
- We regret there is no laundry service ....¹⁶ Sundays.

5 Rewrite the email using the full form of the abbreviations.

File   Edit   View   Insert   Format   Tools   Actions   Help
From: hotelfeliz@hotel.es
To: chinatravel@internet.com
Subject: Confirmation
Attn: Mrs Fong, China Travel
Dear Mrs Fong
Re your request for six double rooms in August. Pls cfm in writing with dates asap.
Rgds
Roberto Gil Reservations Manager Tel: 0034 193 762 51

File   Edit   View   Insert   Format   Tools   Actions   Help
From: hotelfeliz@hotel.es
To: chinatravel@internet.com
Subject: Confirmation
For the attention of Mrs Fong, China Travel
Dear Mrs Fong
....
....
....
Roberto Gil Reservations Manager ....: 0034 193 762 51

6 Find seven more family members in the puzzle. You can read some from left to right (→), some from top to bottom (↓), and some diagonally (↗).

```
X A H X R T X L R X
P X U S S X R E N Y
A P S X T T H U X T
X O B R O T H E R I
U M A X O G A F X R
X O N M V Z R A E X
J O D A U G H T E R
S D X T W I S H X U
F X S H W I F E Y T
X C C O S X I R I X
```

4 Taking restaurant bookings

1 Match the two ways of talking about the time.

1	c	three fifteen	a	twenty past six
2		eight thirty	b	five to five
3		twelve forty-five	c	quarter past three
4		nine ten	d	twenty to three
5		one thirty-five	e	half past eight
6		six twenty	f	ten past nine
7		four fifty-five	g	quarter to one
8		two forty	h	twenty-five to two

2 Read the text. Then make questions and responses from the prompts.

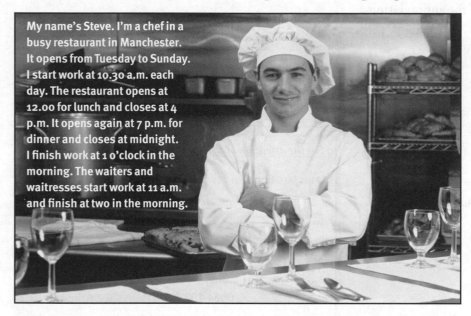

My name's Steve. I'm a chef in a busy restaurant in Manchester. It opens from Tuesday to Sunday. I start work at 10.30 a.m. each day. The restaurant opens at 12.00 for lunch and closes at 4 p.m. It opens again at 7 p.m. for dinner and closes at midnight. I finish work at 1 o'clock in the morning. The waiters and waitresses start work at 11 a.m. and finish at two in the morning.

1 Where / Steve / work?
Where does Steve work?

work / restaurant / Manchester
He works in a restaurant in Manchester.

2 when / restaurant / open?
....

open / Tuesday / Sunday
....

3 What time / open / lunch?
....

open / 12.00
....

4 What time / Steve / start work?
....

start / 10.30
....

5 When / restaurant / close?
....

close / midnight
....

6 When / waiters / finish work?
....

finish work / two in the morning
....

3 Look at Steve's notes for June/July. Then complete sentences 1–8, writing the dates in full.

important dates

Sunday June 23 – finish work

Tuesday June 25 – father's birthday

Friday June 28 – Alan in Manchester

Tuesday July 9 – holiday

Thursday July 16 – home

Saturday July 18 – start at new job

Monday July 20 – opening night

Friday July 24 – pay day

1 Steve finishes work
     on the 23rd of June.

2 His father's birthday is
....

3 His brother, Alan, arrives in Manchester
....

4 They start their holiday
....

5 They finish their holiday
....

6 Steve starts his new job
....

7 The new restaurant opens
....

8 His first pay day is ....
Friday ....

4 Use the clues to find the missing word.

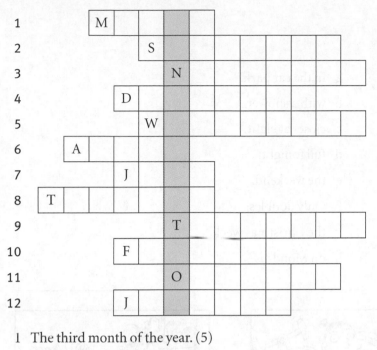

1 The third month of the year. (5)
2 The first day of the weekend. (8)
3 The eleventh month. (8)
4 Christmas Day is 25th .... (8)
5 The middle day of the week. (9)
6 A spring month in Europe. (5)
7 The month between June and August. (4)
8 The day after Monday. (7)
9 The day before Friday. (8)
10 The weekend starts on .... night! (6)
11 The only month beginning with the letter *O*. (7)
12 New Year's Day is 1st .... (7)

5 Underline the correct adverb.

1 I enjoy the theatre.
   I _often_ / *never* go on Saturday night.
2 He works very late.
   He *always* / *rarely* finishes before midnight.
3 Guests always arrive by car.
   They *often* / *never* arrive by train.
4 I love coffee. I *always* / *never* have it for breakfast.
5 Guests *never* / *often* book adjoining rooms
   for their children.
6 My brother lives in the US.
   I *always* / *rarely* see him.
7 *Sometimes* / *Never* I study and *sometimes* / *always*
   I meet my friends.
8 Reception staff *always* / *never* say
   Good morning to guests.
9 The bar isn't busy. It *often* / *never* closes early.

6 Make words from the letters in italics to complete the sentences.

1 Can you meet me at *emithclun*? ....*lunchtime*.......................
2 I *vreen* drink alcohol. ....
3 We often go to Spain for a *laydohi*. ....
4 The new bar *speno* on Saturday. ....
5 The restaurant is *lufyl dekoob* tonight. ....
6 The *tuscmoer* wants a table by the window. ....
7 They *reves* dinner from 7.00 to 10.00. ....
8 We have a *tellacnacion* for tonight. ....
9 My *mayfil* live in Turkey. ....
10 I'd like to make a table *noitservare*, please. ....

5 Giving polite explanations

1 Match the phrases to make polite explanations.

1 | g | I'm afraid we don't have anything left for   a   in the car park.

2 | | I'm sorry, the restaurant is   b   with a shower.

3 | | Unfortunately, we're fully booked at   c   closes at eight.

4 | | I'm sorry, there aren't any parking spaces   d   full tonight.

5 | | I'm afraid we only have a bathroom   e   the weekend.

6 | | Unfortunately, we're closed   f   Only doubles.

7 | | I'm afraid the swimming pool   g   the Christmas week.

8 | | I'm afraid there aren't any twin rooms left.   h   on Mondays.

---

2 Match the requests with the pictures. Then write an appropriate response to the requests.

a | 1 | Room 301, please.

b | | I'd like to go for a swim.

c | | Could I book a double room for tonight?

d | | Can I speak to Nadine in reservations, please?

e | | I'd like a parking space, please.

f | | Do you have a table for 9.30?

g | | Could I speak to the manager?

on holiday

2 ....

closes at 9 p.m.

5 ....

in a meeting

3 ....

full today

6 ....

no answer

1 *I'm sorry, there's no answer from 301.*

fully booked

4 ....

closes at 10 p.m.

7 ....

---

3 Rewrite the verbs in the short form.

1 I am   *I'm*

2 we are   ....

3 she is   ....

4 they are   ....

5 he is not   ....

6 you are not   ....

7 here is   ....

8 there is   ....

9 there is not   ....

10 there are not   ....

11 we cannot   ....

12 I cannot   ....

13 they do not   ....

14 he does not   ....

15 we do not   ....

4 Complete the sentences using the positive or negative short forms of the verbs in brackets.

1 It ....*isn't*.... (be) Friday today. It's Saturday.

2 She .... (do) work on Sundays.
 She works Monday to Saturday.

3 I'm afraid we .... (do) have any rooms left for tonight.

4 Of course, guests .... (can) use the swimming pool today.

5 The manager .... (be) in his office.
 He's on holiday this week.

6 Here's your key. You .... (be) in room 354.

7 We .... (can) take table bookings for the weekend. We're full on Saturday and Sunday.

8 I'm sorry, there .... (be) any adjoining rooms left.

5 Read the email confirming a customer's hotel reservation. Then put the sentences in the correct order.

File Edit View Insert Format Tools Actions Help

Dear Mr Russo

a ☐ I have reserved a parking space in the car park for you,

b ☐ The room has disabled facilities.

c ☐ We are very pleased to confirm your reservation for a double room for three nights from 2nd March.

d [1] Thank you very much for your email.

e ☐ We look forward to welcoming you to the Oriental Palace.

f ☐ and booked a table for two in the restaurant for 7.30 as requested.

Best regards
Lucy Tan
Reservations

6 Complete the crossword using the clues below.

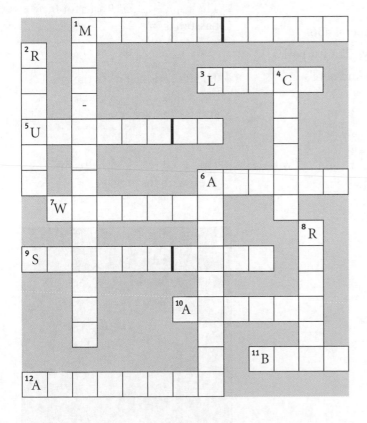

ACROSS

1 Your phone on the move? (6, 5)

3 The meal in the middle of the day. (5)

5 *Can't* in formal, written English. (6, 2)

6 The opposite of *refuse*. (6)

7 Saturday and Sunday. (7)

9 A room for one. (6, 4)

10 Respond to a question. (6)

11 An alternative to a shower. (4)

12 *I'm afraid we're full. We don't have* .... *left for tonight.* (8)

DOWN

1 Around 3 o'clock in the afternoon. (3-9)

2 Say *no* to a request. (6)

4 When you aren't open you're .... (6)

6 The children are in the .... room. (9)

8 *We* .... *that we are unable to confirm your reservation.* (6)

6 Receiving guests

1 Match a word in each column to make a new noun.

1 | d | room   a card
2 | | hair   b phone
3 | | fitness   c address
4 | | registration   d number
5 | | fax   e card
6 | | key   f hours
7 | | home   g centre
8 | | opening   h machine
9 | | mobile   i salon

2 Complete the jumbled dialogue with *my*, *your*, *his*, *her*, *our*, or *their*.

a Yes, we have ......*your*..¹ reservation, Mr Vassili. Please complete this registration card. Could I have ....² passport?

b The fourth floor, OK.
Thank you. We'd like to have dinner in the restaurant this evening. My wife is meeting ....³ sister here.

c Certainly. Carlos, please help Mr and Mrs Vassili with ....⁴ luggage. ....⁵ room number is 436.

d That's right, sir. A parking space is reserved for three days. The car park attendant can help you. ....⁶ name's Michael. And here's ....⁷ key card. ....⁸ room number is 436. It's on the fourth floor.

e Good evening. My name's Stavros Vassili.
You have a reservation for a double room for me and ....⁹ wife.

f Here it is. I also made a reservation for a parking space for ....¹⁰ car.

g Yes, please. A table for three.
Can we have help with ....¹¹ luggage?

h Can I reserve you a table?

3 Now put the sentences in the dialogue in the correct order.

1 | e | 2 | | 3 | | 4 | | 5 | | 6 | | 7 | | 8 | |

4 Complete the flow chart of the check-in procedure.

A guest ......*arrives*......¹ at reception.

↓

The receptionist asks the guest's ....².

↓

The receptionist ....³ the reservation.

↓

The receptionist asks the guest to fill in the ....⁴.

↓

The guest ....⁵ the card including his home address.

↓

The ....⁶ asks for his passport.

↓

The receptionist gives the guest his ....⁷ and room number.

↓

The ....⁸ helps the guest with his luggage.

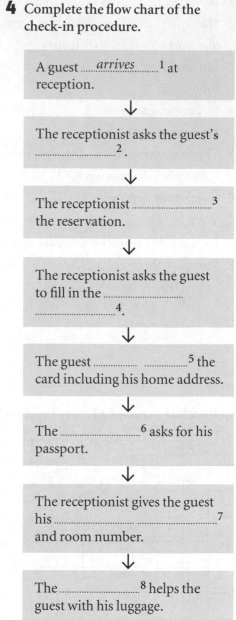

5 Look at the picture. Then read the sentences and underline true or false.

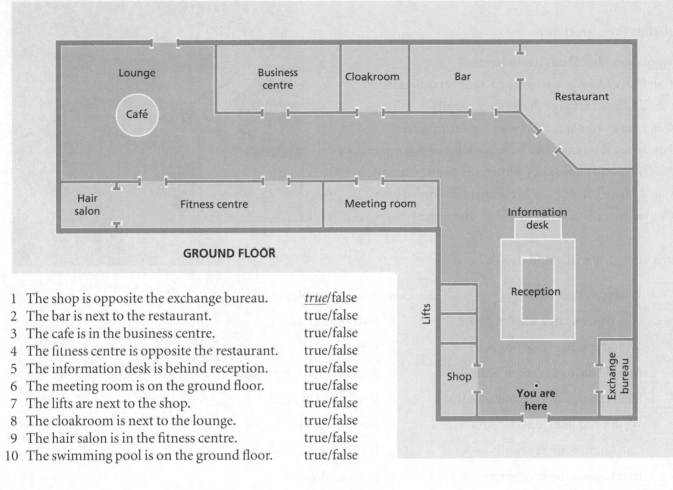

Lounge

Café

Business centre

Cloakroom

Bar

Restaurant

Hair salon

Fitness centre

Meeting room

GROUND FLOOR

Information desk

Reception

Lifts

Shop

You are here

Exchange bureau

1	The shop is opposite the exchange bureau.	_true_/false
2	The bar is next to the restaurant.	true/false
3	The cafe is in the business centre.	true/false
4	The fitness centre is opposite the restaurant.	true/false
5	The information desk is behind reception.	true/false
6	The meeting room is on the ground floor.	true/false
7	The lifts are next to the shop.	true/false
8	The cloakroom is next to the lounge.	true/false
9	The hair salon is in the fitness centre.	true/false
10	The swimming pool is on the ground floor.	true/false

6 Find ten more check-in phrases in the puzzle.
You can read some from left to right (→), some
from top to bottom (↓), and some diagonally (↗).

```
X B L U G G A G E E X S
A R R I V E Y K X A S R
R F X I M K C X U E S E
O F D G X E A S R R X S
O I X U H Y X D P S E E
M L A C X C D I A X O R
N L X F J A V X S I M V
U I P R E R X K S M X A
M N X M A D U L P X R T
B P O R T E R X O L T I
E H Y X I K A R R I X O
R E G I S T R A T I O N
```

7 Serving in the bar

1 Underline the correct form.

1 *Would you like* / *Shall I* ice and lemon?
2 *Can I have* / *Would you like* two large beers, please?
3 *Could I* / *Shall I* charge this to your room?
4 *Can I have* / *Would you like* your key card, please?
5 *Would you like* / *Could we have* sparkling or still mineral water?
6 *Shall I* / *Could I have* a dry white wine and a Margarita?
7 *Could I have* / *Would you like* draught or bottled beer?
8 *Can we have* / *Shall I* our drinks in the garden?

2 Match offers 1–8 with requests a–h.

1 | d | What can I get you?
2 | ☐ | Can I have a large whisky, please.
3 | ☐ | Would you like large or small?
4 | ☐ | Could I have your room number?
5 | ☐ | Shall I charge this to your room?
6 | ☐ | Would you like ice and lemon?
7 | ☐ | Can I have your key card?
8 | ☐ | Can I have a mineral water?

a A large one, please.
b Sparkling or still?
c Here it is.
d A glass of red wine, please.
e Would you like ice?
f No, thanks. I'll pay cash.
g It's 22.
h Just ice, please.

3 Use adjectives to describe the drinks.
Some adjectives can be used more than once.

bottled	double	draught	*dry*
large	medium dry	red	single
small	sparkling	still	
sweet	white		

1 wine *dry* ....
   ....
2 beer ....
   ....
3 spirits ....
   ....
4 water ....

4 Underline the odd one out.

1 dry *still* sweet medium dry
2 soda tonic cocktail ginger ale
3 beer brandy rum vodka
4 port gin sherry vermouth
5 Riesling Chablis Merlot wine
6 orange juice bacardi mineral water coke
7 Guinness Budweiser Margarita San Miguel
8 sparkling large small double

5 Complete the dialogues using the picture prompts.

1 BAR STAFF: What can I get you?
CUSTOMER: *One large beer, and a vodka and tonic* ¹ please.
BAR STAFF: Would you like ....² in the vodka?
CUSTOMER: Yes, please. How much is that?
BAR STAFF: ....³ euros, please.

2 BAR STAFF: Good evening. What can I get you?
CUSTOMER: ....⁴, please.
BAR STAFF: Would you like ....⁵?
CUSTOMER: Dry, please.
BAR STAFF: And would you like ....⁶?
CUSTOMER: A large one, please. How much is that?
BAR STAFF: ....⁷ euros, please.

3 BAR STAFF: What would you like to drink?
CUSTOMER: ....⁸, please.
BAR STAFF: Would you like ....⁹?
CUSTOMER: Still, please.
BAR STAFF: And ....¹⁰?
CUSTOMER: Just a single, please. How much is that?
BAR STAFF: ....¹¹ euros, please.

6 Use the clues to find the missing drink.

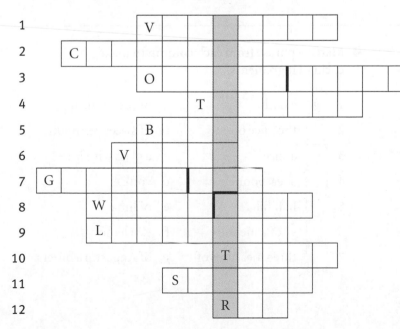

1 A fortified wine. (8)
2 It's usually made in a shaker. (8)
3 A fruit drink. (6,5)
4 The spirit in a Margarita. (7)
5 San Miguel is a type of .... (4)
6 A colourless spirit. (5)
7 A good mixer with brandy or whisky. (6,3)
8 Drink it dry, medium dry, or sweet. (5,4)
9 A lemon soft drink. (8)
10 Gin and .... (5)
11 A fortified wine from Spain. (6)
12 A spirit from the Caribbean. (3)

8 Instructions

1 Use each word once to make cocktail ingredients and equipment.

lemon	sugar	ice	sauce	olive
juice	spoon	shaker	cubes	

1 lime ......*juice*...... 　4 ice .... 　7 slice of ....

2 bar .... 　　5 green .... 　8 Worcester ....

3 cocktail .... 　6 crushed .... 　9 caster ....

---

2 Put the instructions for making a Cuba Libre in the correct order.

a ☐ 　Then pour in 1 measure of light rum.

b ☐ 　Next, garnish with a slice of lime.

c ☐ 　Then fill the glass with cola.

d ☐ *1* 　First, fill a highball glass with ice.

e ☐ 　Finally, serve with a straw.

f ☐ 　Next, add the juice of half a lime and stir well.

---

3 Underline the correct verb.

1 *Mix* / *Squeeze* the liquids with a bar spoon.

2 *Stir* / *Squeeze* some fresh lemon juice.

3 *Shake* / *Strain* the liquid into a glass.

4 *Fill* / *Shake* the cocktail shaker with crushed ice.

5 *Add* / *Serve* 1½ measures of tequila.

6 *Squeeze* / *Pour* the cocktail into a glass.

7 *Serve* / *Chill* with a straw.

8 *Strain* / *Stir* with a bar spoon.

9 *Shake* / *Pour* well to chill the liquids.

10 *Stir* / *Garnish* with a cherry.

4 Match a phrase from each column to make cocktail ingredients.

1	*g*	a dash	a	of caster sugar
2	☐	the juice of	b	of sweet vermouth
3	☐	a slice	c	a glass with ice
4	☐	a teaspoon	d	vodka
5	☐	half fill	e	of lime
6	☐	¾ of a measure	f	½ a lemon
7	☐	three measures of	g	of Angostura bitters

5 Read the ingredients and look at the pictures. Then write the instructions for making a Daiquiri.

DAIQUIRI

3 measures light rum

1 measure lemon juice

1 teaspoon caster sugar

crushed ice

slice of lemon

1 *First, fill a cocktail shaker with crushed ice.*

2 ....

3 ....

4 ....

5 ....

6 ....

7 ....

6 Complete the crossword using the clues below.

ACROSS

4   It chills your drink. (7, 3)

6   You can .... a cocktail with cherries, olives, and lemon. (7)

7   A rum-based cocktail. (4, 5)

9   Finally, stir with a .... (3, 5)

10 Whisky, vermouth, and bitters make a .... (9)

11 The liquid of a small green citrus fruit. (4, 5)

DOWN

1   You serve a cocktail in this. (5)

2   A popular US cocktail. (9)

3   First take a .... (8,6)

5   A popular tequila cocktail. (9)

8   Angostura .... (7)

9 Taking a food order

1 Make words from the letters in italics to complete the menu.

Starter menu

🍴 basil and *atotmo*[1] soup
　　　tomato

🍴 red *nonio*[2] tart
　　..

🍴 *shomurom*[3] pâté
　　..

🍴 *kucd's*[4] liver pâté
　　..

🍴 *slemou*[5] marinière
　　..

🍴 goat's cheese *dasal*[6]
　　..

*　　* ✳ ✳ ✳

---

2 Name the food items and add them to one of the menus. Some items are on two menus.

Breakfast menu

1 | c | croissant
2 | | ....
3 | | ....
4 | | ....

Light lunch menu

5 | | ....
6 | | ....
7 | | ....

Dinner menu

8 | | ....
9 | | ....
10 | | ....
11 | | ....
12 | | ....

---

3 Find five more mistakes and correct them. Tick (✔) the correct sentences.

1　Would you like to order ~~the~~ aperitif? ....*an*..............

2　I'd like a Daiquiri, please. ....

3　Would you like to see the dessert menu? ....

4　I'd like to book the table for five on Saturday evening. ....

5　What's a soup of the day? ....

6　We'd like a beer and two Cokes, please. ....

7　Would you like to see a wine list? ....

8　I'd like an egg sandwich and the pot of tea, please. ....

9　I'll have half the bottle of Merlot, please. ....

10　Would you like a double or a twin room? ....

4 Label the words: *C* for countable nouns, *U* for uncountable nouns, and *C/U* for nouns that can be both.

beer *C/U*	bread *U*
tea	glass of wine
water	double whisky
starter	coffee
toast	money
aperitif	cocktail
fish	milk
luggage	bottle of water
ice	taxi
time	parking space
help	

5 Make questions and answers using *a/an* or *some*.

1 Would you / wine?

Just glass / Chablis.

Would you like some wine?

Just a glass of Chablis.

2 Would you / aperitif?

Yes / gin and tonic.

....

....

3 Can I / change / money here?

Yes. There's / exchange bureau / lobby.

....

....

4 Could we / mineral water?

Would you / large bottle / small bottle?

....

....

5 Could I / sandwich / orange juice?

Would you / ice / your orange juice?

....

....

6 Could you / call / taxi?

Certainly. Would you / help / luggage?

....

....

6 Put the sentences in the dialogue in the correct order.

a ☐ WAITER: Here's your table. Can I take your coats?

b ☐ MAN: Yes. I'd like a whisky sour and my wife would like a vodka and tonic.

c ☐ WAITER: Brezina. Table for two at 8 o'clock.
Come this way and I'll show you to your table.

d ☐ MAN: Thank you.

e ☐ WAITER: Here's the menu and wine list. Would you like an aperitif?

f ☐ MAN: Thank you.

g ☐ WAITER: Whisky sour, vodka and tonic. Fine.
And the soup of the day is French onion.

h ☐ MAN: Good evening. We booked a table for two.
The name is Brezina.

i [1] WAITER: Good evening.

7 Find ten more meat and fish words in the puzzle. You can read some from left to right (→), some from top to bottom (↑), and some diagonally (↗).

```
G X O K M X I F P E X S
I L R X I C R X F R U X
X O B M M O N K F I S H
P R X A B O L K X V I N
C X H S M X U L K Z B X
H F I L L E T S T E A K
A P A A X O D X I N C M
L S N M U X A R W I O X
I J X B E E F A S X N U
B E C O X J R X I M E X
U X E B S P X T U X L E
T O M X C H I C K E N O
```

1 Match a word in each column to make popular desserts.

1	_f_	Vanilla	a	tart
2		Blackcurrant	b	pudding
3		Crème	c	salad
4		Chocolate	d	with chocolate sauce
5		Profiteroles	e	mousse
6		Fruit	f	ice cream
7		Summer	g	brûlée
8		French apple	h	sorbet

2 Read the sentences and underline true or false.

1 Cheddar is a hard cheese from Britain. _true_/false
2 Roquefort is a blue cheese from Italy. true/false
3 Manchego is a soft cheese from Spain. true/false
4 Dolcelatte is a soft blue cheese from Italy. true/false
5 Gouda is a hard cheese from the Netherlands. true/false
6 Danish blue is a hard cheese from Denmark. true/false
7 Gruyère is a hard cheese from France. true/false
8 Mozzarella is a soft cheese from Italy. true/false
9 Camembert and Brie are soft cheeses from France. true/false
10 Parmesan is a soft cheese from Italy. true/false

3 Label the countries 1–10 on the map of the world.

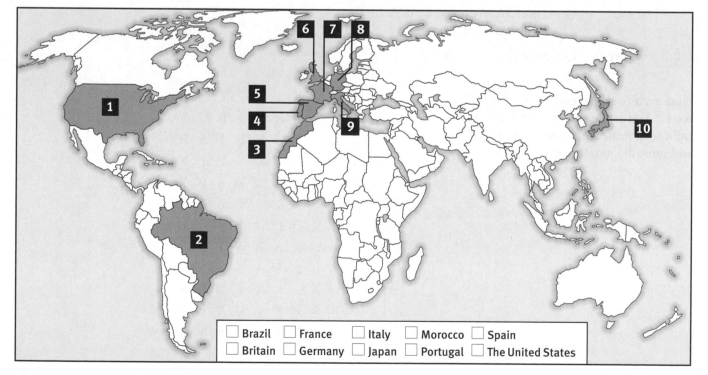

Brazil ☐ France ☐ Italy ☐ Morocco ☐ Spain ☐
Britain ☐ Germany ☐ Japan ☐ Portugal ☐ The United States ☐

4 Complete the table of countries, nationalities, and languages.

Country	Nationality	Language
Brazil	*Brazilian*	*Portuguese*
Britain		
France		
Germany		
Italy	*Italian*	
Japan		
Morocco		*Arabic*
Portugal		
Spain		
The United States	*American*	

5 Complete the dialogue using *some* or *any*.

MAN: Do you have ....*any*........[1] ice cream?

STAFF: Yes. There's vanilla, chocolate, and strawberry.

MAN: I'd like ....[2] chocolate and vanilla, please. What about you, Kate?

WOMAN: Do you have ....[3] fresh fruit salad?

STAFF: I'm afraid we don't have ....[4] left. Would you like ....[5] fresh fruit instead?

WOMAN: That would be nice. Thank you.

STAFF: Would you like ....[6] more wine? No, thanks.

STAFF: OK. Would you like ....[7] coffee after your dessert?

MAN: I don't want ....[8], thanks. Kate?

WOMAN: An espresso, please.

6 Use the clues to find the missing dessert.

1 A small black fruit. (12)
2 A blue cheese from Denmark. (6,4)
3 A hard Spanish cheese. (8)
4 The flavour of white ice cream. (7)
5 A small, soft, red fruit. (9)
6 A popular American/British dessert. (5,3)
7 A soft cheese from France. (9)
8 The cheese used on pizzas. (10)
9 Fresh fruit dessert. (5,5)
10 A good dessert for a hot day. (3,5)

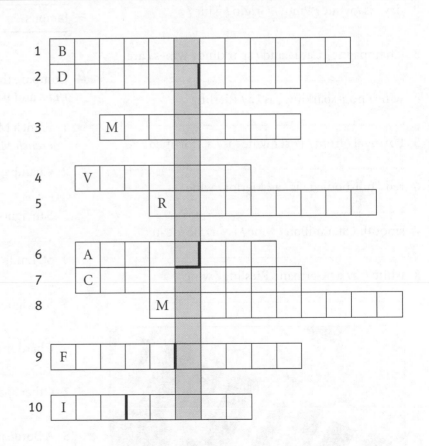

1 B

2 D

3 M

4 V

5 R

6 A

7 C

8 M

9 F

10 I

11 Talking about wine

1 Match adjectives 1–8 with their opposites a–h.

1	d	good	a	unpopular
2		cheap	b	white
3		light	c	sweet
4		smooth	d	bad
5		dry	e	non-sparkling
6		sparkling	f	rough
7		red	g	expensive
8		popular	h	full-bodied

2 Put the words in the correct order.

1 Italian / light / wine / Frascati / is / a / white
Frascati is a light Italian white wine.

2 dry / is / white / Pinot / Grigio / wine / a

....

3 Champagne / Cava / and / sparkling / wines / are

....

4 wine / non-sparkling / is / a / Riesling

....

5 Portugal / from / Port / wine / is / a / fortified

....

6 red / full-bodied / is / a / Merlot / wine

....

7 smooth / St. Emilion / wine / is / a / Bordeaux

....

8 white / is / a / German / Riesling / wine

....

3 Complete the table with the comparative forms of the adjectives.

Adjective	Comparative
cheap	*cheaper*
expensive	*more expensive*
dry	
sweet	
smooth	
rough	
good	
bad	
full-bodied	
light	
famous	

4 Compare the different wines using *-er than*, *more …than*, and *not as … as*.

1 French Merlot / expensive / Chilean Merlot
French Merlot is more expensive than Chilean Merlot.

2 Champagne / famous / Cava and Sekt

....

3 Sauvignon Blanc / sweet / Pinot Grigio

....

4 St. Emilion / smooth / a cheap Bordeaux wine

....

5 Sauvignon Blanc / dry / Chardonnay

....

6 Chardonnay / not light / Frascati

....

7 Other sparkling wines / not expensive / Champagne

....

8 A Bordeaux wine / full-bodied / a young Beaujolais

....

9 A good claret / good / a cheap red wine

....

5 Answer the questions using the map.

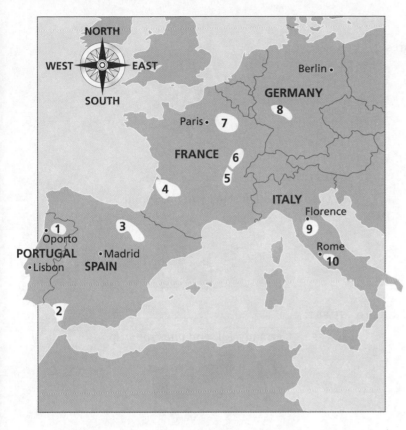

1 Where does port come from?
   *Port comes from **the north of** Portugal.*

2 Where is sherry produced?
   ....

3 Where is the Rioja region?
   ....

4 Where is Bordeaux produced?
   ....

5 Where does Beaujolais come from?
   ....

6 Where is the Burgundy wine region?
   ....

7 Where is Champagne produced?
   ....

8 Where does Riesling come from?
   ....

9 Where is the Chianti region?
   ....

10 Where is Frascati produced?
   ....

6 Complete the crossword using the clues below.

ACROSS

2 A restaurant's wine selection. (4, 4)

4 *This wine tastes bad. Perhaps it's*
   .... (6)

5 St. Emilion is a .... wine. (8)

7 The country where Chianti and Frascati
   are produced. (5)

8 The most famous sparkling wine. (9)

9 Pinot Grigio is a ....
   white wine. (3)

DOWN

1 This red wine is not light.
   It's .... (4-6)

3 A good Bordeaux is full-bodied and
   .... (6)

6 A piece of paper attached to a wine bottle,
   with information about it. (5)

10 You serve red wine at ....
   temperature. (4)

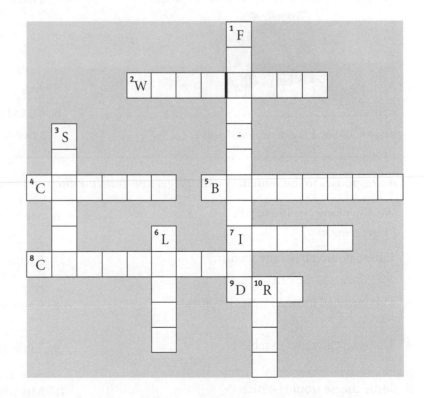

1 Use *Could I/Could we* to make requests from the pictures.
Then underline the correct form in the response.

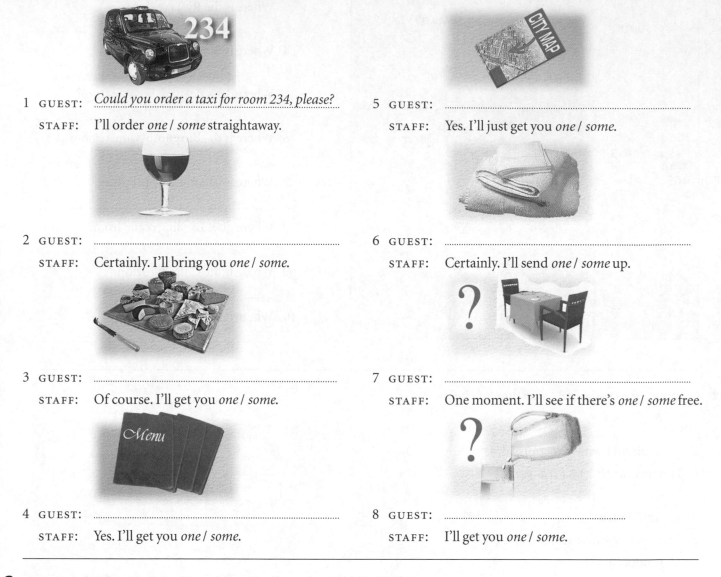

1 GUEST: *Could you order a taxi for room 234, please?*
STAFF: I'll order <u>one</u> / some straightaway.

2 GUEST: ....
STAFF: Certainly. I'll bring you one / some.

3 GUEST: ....
STAFF: Of course. I'll get you one / some.

4 GUEST: ....
STAFF: Yes. I'll get you one / some.

5 GUEST: ....
STAFF: Yes. I'll just get you one / some.

6 GUEST: ....
STAFF: Certainly. I'll send one / some up.

7 GUEST: ....
STAFF: One moment. I'll see if there's one / some free.

8 GUEST: ....
STAFF: I'll get you one / some.

2 Make responses to the sentences with *I'll get some/ one/ another/ some more.*

1 We don't have any bread left.
I'll get some more.

2 Table 6 doesn't have any menus.
....

3 This bottle of mineral water is warm.
....

4 There isn't any salt on table 11.
....

5 Some cheese would be nice.
....

6 My knife is dirty.
....

7 Excuse me. The milk is nearly finished.
....

8 Can I see the dessert menu?
....

9 Table 3 would like extra toast.
....

10 Mrs Kruger wants a pen for the bill.
....

3 Put the sentences in the telephone dialogue in the correct order.

a ☐ RECEPTION: I'll ask housekeeping to get you some more.

b ☐ GUEST: We'd like a bottle of mineral water, two glasses, and a selection of vegetarian sandwiches. Thank you very much.

c ☐ RECEPTION: In 304? I'm very sorry. I'll speak to them straightaway.

d ☐ GUEST: Thank you. One last thing. Can I order drinks and sandwiches from you?

e 1 RECEPTION: Reception. How can I help you?

f ☐ GUEST: OK, I'll wait for housekeeping before I take a shower.
Also, I'm sorry to complain but the people in 304 are very noisy.

g ☐ RECEPTION: Certainly. I'll send some toiletries up to your room.

h ☐ GUEST: Thank you. And our bathroom towels are very wet.

i ☐ RECEPTION: If you give me your order, I'll pass it on to room service.

j ☐ GUEST: Hello. It's Mrs Beneto in room 303. Can we have some more soap and shower gel, please?

---

4 Complete the words.

THE CUSTOMER CARE CODE

- Always *w e l c o m e*[1] customers with a smile.
- A ___ s ___ e ___ [2] the phone quickly.
- Apo ___ o ___ i ___ e[3] for any delay in answering the phone.
- Always be p ___ l ___ t ___ [4] and f ___ i ___ n ___ ly[5].
- Use the customer's n ___ m ___ [6] when you talk to them.
- Take spe ___ i ___ l[7] care of people with particular needs.
- Be p ___ t ___ e ___ t[8] and h ___ l ___ ful[9].
- Don't keep people w ___ i ___ ing[10] long.
- ☺ ___ ___ ___ ___ ___ ___ [11] at waiting guests.

5 Find eleven more uncountable nouns in the puzzle. You can read some from left to right (→), some from top to bottom (↑), and some diagonally (↗)

```
X R I X T O E L E X S A
L I X S C N X M R H N X
X K A X I Z I E X O L K
G O S (W A T E R) I M X B
T R A E X U N T X E F E
X A L U G G A G E W O X
E X T I X M I N C O X P
N J X L R O X K A R E X
X A D O U N O U X K S S
D X F B R E A D L X A T
O N N X M Y A I X O G E
I C E T H X M A Y T X B
```

13 Describing dishes

1 Match the food with the ingredients.

1 [b] Penne arrabbiata
2 [   ] Mixed seafood
3 [   ] Hollandaise sauce
4 [   ] Salmon coulibiac
5 [   ] Bearnaise sauce
6 [   ] Summer pudding
7 [   ] Meringues

a thin slices of white bread, raspberries, and sugar
b chilli, tomatoes, garlic, basil, pine nuts, and pasta
c egg whites, and icing sugar
d tarragon, shallots, vinegar, dry white wine, egg yolks, butter, and salt and pepper
e layers of rice, onions, mushrooms, salmon, and hard-boiled eggs in puff pastry
f egg yolks, lemon juice, butter, and salt and pepper
g half a lobster, king prawns, scallops, and mussels

2 Answer the questions using the prompts.

1 What is ice cream made from?
   • cream/eggs/sugar
   It's made from cream, eggs, and sugar.

2 What does a continental breakfast consist of?
   • fruit juice/croissant or bread/jam/butter/coffee

3 What does the mixed seafood dish contain?
   • lobster/prawns/scallops/mussels

4 What does a Margarita consist of?
   • tequila/triple sec/lime and lemon juice/ice

5 What is summer pudding made from?
   • bread strips/raspberries/sugar

6 What vegetables does the vegetarian bake contain?
   • aubergines/tomatoes/onions/broccoli/mushrooms

7 What are pancakes made from?
   • eggs/milk/flour

8 What does the chef's salad consist of?
   • green salad/tuna/olives/tomatoes

9 What's the salad dressing made from?
   • olive oil/wine vinegar/mustard

10 What does the penne arrabiata consist of?
    • pasta/chilli/tomatoes/garlic/basil/pine nuts

3 Rewrite the instructions in the Passive for how to make a Summer pudding.

   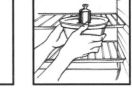 

1 Remove the crusts from some thin slices of white bread.
   The crusts are removed from some thin slices of white bread.

2 Cut each slice into three or four pieces.

3 Put some of the bread strips around a pudding bowl.

....

4 Stew the raspberries in the sugar for a few minutes.

....

5 Add the fruit and some of the juice to the pudding bowl.

....

6 Cover the fruit with more bread strips.

....

7 Pour over the remaining juice.

....

8 Put a weight on top of the bowl and place it in the refrigerator.

....

4 Rewrite the Passive sentences as instructions for how to lay a place setting.

1 A clean tablecloth is put on the table.
Put a clean tablecloth on the table.

2 A knife and fork are put in the plate position.

....

3 A napkin is folded and placed on a side plate.

....

4 A dessert spoon and fork are brought with the dessert menu.

....

5 A wine glass is placed above the soup spoon position.

....

6 Salt and pepper are put in the centre of the table.

....

7 A flower arrangement and a candle are placed by the salt and pepper.

....

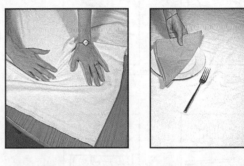

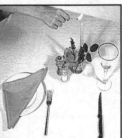

5 Use the clues to find the missing wine, perfect with seafood.

1 A shellfish starter. (8)
2 The waiter brings this and removes the meat fork. (4,4)
3 This large shellfish changes colour when cooked. (7)
4 A good light sauce for fish. (11)
5,6 This fish dish is usually served as a starter. (6,6)
7 Another piece of cutlery for eating fish. (4,5)
8 A popular *royal* shellfish for starters and main courses. (4,5)
9 A sauce often served with cod. (6)

14 Dealing with complaints

1 Match the pictures with the adjectives.

a	empty	e	corked
b	torn	f	off
c	overcooked	g	undercooked
d	*full*	h	flat

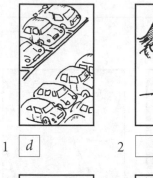

1 [d]   2 [ ]

3 [ ]   4 [ ]

5 [ ]   6 [ ]

7 [ ]   8 [ ]

2 Complete the complaints with the best answer.

1 You've given us the ....*wrong*........ rooms. We asked for adjoining doubles.
   a bad   **b** right   **c** *wrong*   **d** good

2 Sorry, this bread is really ....
   a stale   **b** fresh   **c** good   **d** flat

3 This is room 409. Our bathroom is absolutely ....
   a unmade   **b** filthy   **c** dirty   **d** dusty

4 These vegetables are really .... They have no taste at all.
   a new   **b** vinegary   **c** cold   **d** tasteless

5 Excuse me. I can't eat this soup – it's too ....
   a warm   **b** tasteless   **c** salty   **d** flat

6 Are you the reception manager? One of your staff was very .... to me today.
   a rude   **b** friendly   **c** bad   **d** dirty

7 The TV in our room is ....
   a dusty   **b** full   **c** broken   **d** torn

8 This meat is so .... that it's difficult to cut.
   a tasteless   **b** tough   **c** cold   **d** stale

9 Our room is very .... because of the street traffic. We can't sleep.
   a full   **b** dirty   **c** hot   **d** noisy

10 This wine tastes .... I think it's corked.
   a vinegary   **b** salty   **c** tasteless   **d** flat

3 Match responses a–j with the complaints in exercise 2.

a [3] I'm very sorry. I'll speak to housekeeping straight away.

b [ ] I'm sorry. I'll speak to the wine waiter who will replace it for you.

c [ ] I'm sorry. Can I get you a salad instead?

d [ ] I'm sorry. I'll change them straightaway.

e [ ] I'll ask maintenance to sort it out for you immediately.

f [ ] I'm sorry. Would you like to choose another soup?

g [ ] I'm sorry. I'll get you some fresh bread.

h [ ] I can move you to a room at the back of the hotel.

i [ ] I do apologize. I'll speak to the person concerned.

j [ ] I'm sorry. I'll speak to the chef. Would you like something else?

4 Complete the sentences with the verbs in the Past Simple tense.

1 They ....*ordered*.... (order) a bottle of red wine.

2 The waitress .... (open) the bottle of champagne.

3 The waiter .... (take) their order.

4 The guests .... (arrive) at 10 p.m.

5 The restaurant manager .... (speak) to the chef about the complaint.

6 The manager .... (look into) the complaint about his staff.

7 The receptionist .... (smile) at the new guests.

8 The guests .... (leave) after breakfast.

9 The guest .... (give) the waiter her key card.

10 They .... (reserve) a table for dinner at 8 p.m.

11 They .... (meet) their friends after work.

12 The bar server .... (shake) the cocktail shaker.

5 Complete the letter with the verbs in the Past Simple tense.

give	*receive*	not be	not want
book	be	wait	speak
take	arrive	make	complain

Dear Sir/Madam

I would like to complain about the recent poor service which I .....*received*.....¹ at your hotel.

When we ....² on Saturday afternoon, our room ....³ ready for us. Then the receptionist ....⁴ us the wrong room without a balcony or shower. She ....⁵ to change the room for us but I insisted.

I ....⁶ a table for dinner when I ....⁷ our room reservation but we ....⁸ more than half an hour for a table. The waiter ....⁹ our order and we then waited another thirty minutes for our food. The food was not good. The meat ....¹⁰ tough and the vegetables watery and overcooked. I ....¹¹ to the waiter and then I ....¹² with the restaurant manager, who was unsympathetic.

I remain an unhappy customer.

Yours faithfully

6 Complete the crossword using the clues below.

ACROSS

4 No taste at all. (9)
6 Really dirty. (6)
7 Meat that is difficult to eat. (5)
11 Wine that is too old. (8)
12 Too much salt. (5)
13 Too much H_2O. (6)
14 The opposite of *polite*. (4)

DOWN

1 Cooked for too long. (10)
2 Covered in dust. (5)
3 Green beans can be like this. (7)
5 Champagne with no sparkle. (4)
8 Another word for *loud*. (5)
9 Not working. (6)
10 Certainly not fresh. (5)

15 Jobs and workplaces

1 Look at the pictures. Then complete the sentences with jobs, and *responsible to* or *responsible for*.

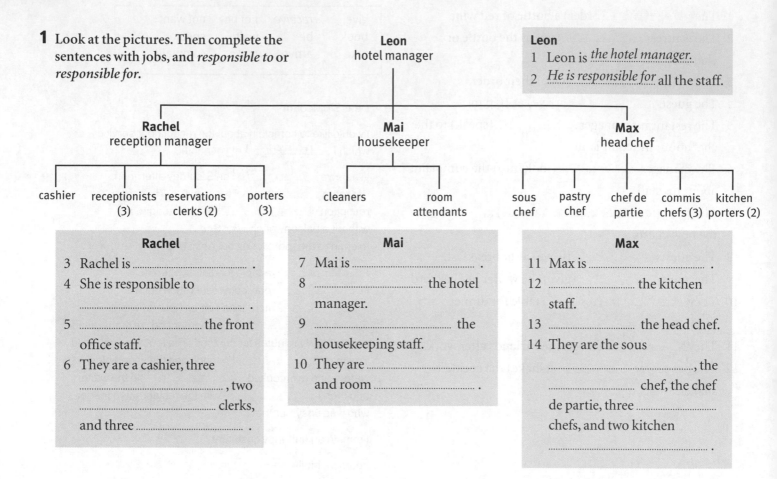

Leon
hotel manager

Leon
1 Leon is *the hotel manager.*
2 *He is responsible for* all the staff.

Rachel
reception manager

cashier | receptionists (3) | reservations clerks (2) | porters (3)

Mai
housekeeper

cleaners | room attendants

Max
head chef

sous chef | pastry chef | chef de partie | commis chefs (3) | kitchen porters (2)

Rachel
3 Rachel is ....
4 She is responsible to ....
5 .... the front office staff.
6 They are a cashier, three .... , two .... clerks, and three ....

Mai
7 Mai is ....
8 .... the hotel manager.
9 .... the housekeeping staff.
10 They are .... and room ....

Max
11 Max is ....
12 .... the kitchen staff.
13 .... the head chef.
14 They are the sous .... , the .... chef, the chef de partie, three .... chefs, and two kitchen ....

---

2 Match the jobs with the responsibilities.

		JOB		RESPONSIBILITY
1	c	reception manager	a	menus and the kitchen
2		restaurant manager	b	luggage
3		housekeeper	c	front office
4		head chef	d	guests' questions and requests
5		cashier	e	baking bread and croissants
6		receptionist	f	bedrooms and linen
7		reservations clerk	g	helping the sous chef
8		porter	h	the restaurant staff rotas
9		room attendants	i	reservations by phones and email
10		pastry chef	j	money and bills
11		commis chef	k	preparing vegetables
12		kitchen porter	l	cleaning rooms and making beds

3 Complete the sentences with *this/that* or *these/those*.

1 Right. ......*This*...... menu here is today's menu.

2 Look at this menu. .... are the dishes I want you to prepare.

3 ....'s tomorrow's menu over on the board.

4 .... are tomorrow's dishes over there.

5 .... desserts here are ready for the dining room.

6 Those on .... worktop aren't finished yet.

7 Could you pass me .... bottle? The one on the shelf.

8 I'll serve .... dishes here if you take ....

9 Here you are, sir. .... is today's lunch menu.

10 Excuse me. Who are .... people over there?

---

4 Complete the sentences with the best answer.

1 Put the dirty plates into the ......*dishwasher*...... .
  a cupboard   **b** bin   **c** blender   **d** *dishwasher*

2 You use a .... to make meringue.
  a blender   **b** whisk   **c** knife   **d** sieve

3 When you make a tart you cook it in the ....
  a deep fryer   **b** grill   **c** oven   **d** frying pan

4 Eggs are boiled on the ....
  a grill   **b** oven   **c** hob   **d** saucepan

5 French fries are cooked in the ....
  a oven   **b** frying pan   **c** deep fat fryer   **d** food processor

6 We make soup using the liquid in the ....
  a stockpot   **b** blender   **c** refrigerator   **d** saucepan

7 Food is kept warm under the ....
  a oven   **b** heat lamps   **c** grill   **d** hob

8 Each chef has their own ....
  a cupboard   **b** oven   **c** worktop   **d** work station

9 The waiters make toast in the ....
  a grill   **b** toaster   **c** heat lamp   **d** blender

10 The kitchen porters .... the kitchen knives every day.
  a sharpen   **b** wash   **c** clean   **d** cut

5 Find nine more pieces of kitchen equipment or kitchenware in the puzzle. You can read some from left to right (→), some from top to bottom (↓), and some diagonally (↗).

```
R  S  T  O  C  K  P  O  T  N  O  X
E  X  S  A  U  C  E  P  A  N  X  K
F  I  H  X  R  T  X  P  M  O  I  D
R  S  O  L  X  T  G  E  N  X  B  I
I  X  B  L  E  N  D  E  R  D  A  S
G  R  X  K  I  X  V  E  L  X  O  H
E  X  A  Y  X  O  R  V  X  M  E  W
R  E  R  X  B  C  X  Q  U  I  X  A
A  F  B  A  K  I  N  G  T  I  N  S
T  X  A  M  O  X  K  I  L  X  C  H
O  W  H  X  O  L  X  S  T  O  X  E
R  X  J  F  X  T  O  A  S  T  E  R
```

1 Complete the sentences with the correct verb.

1 We have to julienne the carrots and ....*chop*.......... the onions.

   a cut   **b** prepare   **c** *chop*   **d** break

2 The kitchen porters .... the potatoes before boiling them.

   a slice   **b** strain   **c** beat   **d** pour

3 You have to .... the broccoli and cauliflower into florets before boiling.

   a prepare   **b** fold   **c** stir   **d** break

4 .... the egg whites together to make meringue.

   a whisk   **b** cut   **c** blend   **d** stir

5 .... the sauce to stop it sticking to the pan.

   a whip   **b** stir   **c** break   **d** beat

6 .... the cream to make a topping for the desserts.

   a beat   **b** blend   **c** whip   **d** stir

7 .... the fruit and chop it into pieces to make a fruit salad.

   a scrape   **b** peel   **c** slice   **d** cut

8 .... the meat thinly and put it on the plates.

   a whip   **b** prepare   **c** scrape   **d** slice

9 The kitchen staff always .... their hands in the hand basin.

   a clean   **b** wash   **c** dry   **d** sweep

10 The kitchen porters .... and wash the floors every day.

   a sweep   **b** make   **c** dust   **d** prepare

2 Match the instructions with the pictures.

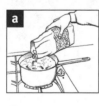 a

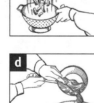 b

 c

 d

 e

f

1 | *b* | Strain the pasta into a colander.

2 | | Boil a large pan of water.

3 | | Add the sauce and serve immediately.

4 | | Boil for 7 or 8 minutes until the pasta is al dente.

5 | | Add salt and a dash of oil to the water.

6 | | Put the pasta in the boiling water.

3 Now put the instructions in the correct order.

| 2 | | | | | |

4 Use each verb once to complete the room attendant's instructions.

empty	clean	strip
replace	*open*	check
put	make	
take	clean and dust	

1 ....*Open*.......... the windows.

2 .... the beds.

3 .... the dirty linen in the laundry bag.

4 .... clean sheets and pillow cases from the trolley.

5 .... the beds.

6 .... the room.

7 .... the bathroom.

8 .... all the bins.

9 .... the toiletries in the bathroom.

10 .... the minibar, lights, and electrical equipment.

5 Make sentences with *mustn't* or *don't/doesn't have to.*

1 Guests / pay for the car park
Guests don't have to pay for the car park.

2 You / overcook the vegetables

3 Guests / check out until 12 noon

4 Akiko / work on Thursdays. It's her day off.

5 Staff / wash their hands in the food preparation sinks

6 Room attendants / change the towels every day

7 Staff / smoke in the kitchen

8 Staff / be rude to customers

9 The kitchen porters / scrape the new potatoes

10 Reception staff / keep guests waiting

6 Complete the text with *must* or *have to.*

ROBBIE AND DIRK work in the kitchen. They *have to* 1 prepare the vegetables for lunch every morning. Also, they .... 2 chop onions and peel carrots. They .... 3 wash their hands in the hand basin before touching food. They .... 4 wash the kitchen floors every day and they .... 5 clean the bins regularly. They .... 6 remember to put the rubbish in the correct bins for food or general rubbish.

LYN AND PETRA are room attendants. They .... 7 make the beds and clean the rooms every day. They .... 8 replace the bathroom toiletries and they .... 9 check the minibar and the light bulbs. They .... 10 make sure that everything in the bathroom is very clean.

7 Use the clues to find out how clean the kitchens and bathrooms must be.

1 Kitchen staff must always wash their hands in this. (4,5)

2 The pastry chef uses this to roll out pastry. (7, 3)

3 Useful for making meringue. (7, 5)

4 Another word for kitchen *tools*. (8)

5 Shampoo, shower gel, soap, and toothpaste are .... (10)

6 Strain your vegetables in this. (8)

7 Guests sometimes leave these on the bathroom floor. (6)

8 Kitchen porters put this in the bins. (7)

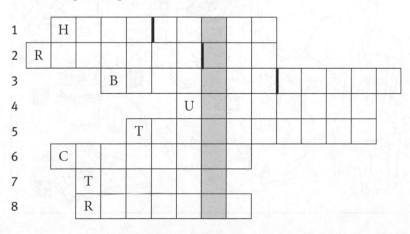

1 Match a phrase in each column to make room service requests.

1 | g | Coffee and cheese
2 | ☐ | A continental
3 | ☐ | A taxi
4 | ☐ | Two beefburgers
5 | ☐ | A bottle of French Merlot
6 | ☐ | A pot of tea for three
7 | ☐ | Some fresh towels
8 | ☐ | Two more

a pillows for room 34.
b and three wine glasses.
c and some pastries.
d for the bathroom in 167.
e for 6 p.m.
f and some French fries.
g sandwiches for two.
h breakfast for one.

2 Complete the sentences with the correct form of *need*.

1 Housekeeping ....*needs to*.... service all the rooms.
2 Mr Delporte .... a parking space.
3 He .... park his car in the car park.
4 Room 34 .... two more pillows.
5 The duty manager .... follow up the complaint.
6 The guests .... a taxi for 6 p.m.
7 Reception .... order the taxi for room 721.
8 The hotel .... confirm the booking.
9 The little boy .... a doctor.
10 Tables 6 and 8 .... a bottle of sparkling mineral water.

3 Look at the picture. Then use the verbs to make sentences about what needs doing.

refill	wash	make
repair	clean	iron/press
change	answer	empty
dry clean		

1 *The skirt needs dry cleaning.*
2 ....
3 ....
4 ....
5 ....
6 ....
7 ....
8 ....
9 ....
10 ....

4 Make responses to the requests.

1 Where can I get a haircut?
 • hair salon / opposite reception
 There's a hair salon opposite reception.

2 What time does the salon close?
 • close / 5 p.m.
 ....

3 Where can I change some money?
 • exchange bureau / ground floor
 ....

4 Where can I change my flight?
 • travel agency / next door to hotel
 ....

5 I need my suit cleaned.
 • send housekeeping / your room
 ....

6 Where can I get theatre tickets?
 • ask / doorman / theatre-booking service
 ....

7 My wife is feeling ill. She needs a doctor.
 • call one / immediately
 ....

8 Can you get me a taxi to the airport?
 • order one / straightaway
 ....

---

5 Complete the crossword using the clues below.

ACROSS
4 A tasty bread starter. (6,5)
6 Non-alcoholic drink. (4,5)
8 This is good to eat on hot day. (3, 5)
10 Espresso, latte, or cappuccino. (6)
11 China, Indian, herb, or fruit. (3)
12 A nice snack for a sweet tooth. (6)
13 A drink made with fresh fruit. (5,5)

DOWN
1 Deep-fried potato sticks. (6, 5)
2 Many restaurants specialize in this Italian dish. (5)
3 A popular US fast food. (4, 6)
5 Two pieces of bread with food between them. (8)
7 A meal made from eggs. (8)
9 A liquid dish. (4)

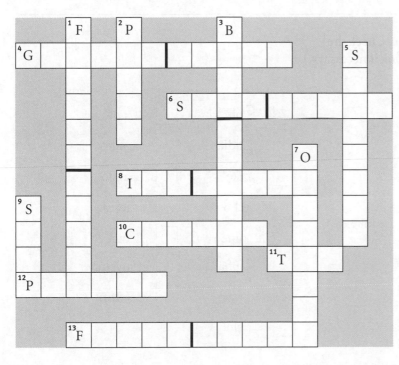

18 Taking difficult phone calls

1 Underline the correct verb.

1 Do you *speak* / *talk* English?

2 I didn't *spell* / *catch* your name.

3 Did you *say* / *tell* K for Kilo?

4 Could you *speak up* / *talk down*, please?

5 I'm sorry, I can't *listen* / *hear* you.

6 We *get* / *have* a very bad line.

7 Can you *say* / *spell* that for me, please?

8 Could you *repeat* / *speak* that, please?

9 Can you *speak* / *say* more slowly?

10 Can you *speak* / *say* those dates again?

2 Put the sentences in the telephone dialogue in the correct order.

a	☐	RECEPTION:	Brett. Could you spell that for me, please?
b	☐	WOMAN:	It's 0041 962 4035.
c	☐	RECEPTION:	Yes, madam. When is it for?
d	☐	WOMAN:	Hello. I'd like to make a reservation.
e	☐	RECEPTION:	I'm sorry, could you repeat the date please?
f	☐	WOMAN:	No, I didn't. I said B. B for Bravo.
g	☐	RECEPTION:	Thank you. Your reservation is made. Would you please confirm in writing by fax or email?
h	☐	WOMAN:	B-R-E-T-T.
i	☐	RECEPTION:	OK. Thank you. So, the 18th to the 23rd of August, a family room. What name is it, please?
j	☐	WOMAN:	It's Brett. Mr and Mrs Brett, and our child.
k	1	RECEPTION:	Good morning, Coral Beach Hotel. Can I help you?
l	☐	WOMAN:	I said from the 18th of August.
m	☐	RECEPTION:	Sorry, did you say P-R ... ?
n	☐	WOMAN:	It's for five nights from the 18th of August. A family room, please.
o	☐	RECEPTION:	B for Bravo. I see. And could I have a contact number?

3 Use letters 1–15 to complete the correct phone code. (Check the Telephone alphabet on page 110 of the Student's Book if necessary.) Then practise saying them.

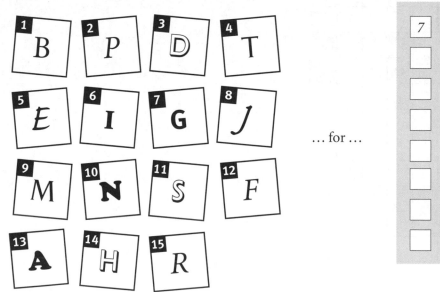

... for ...

7 *G*olf	☐ ......apa
☐ ......ndia	☐ ......uliet
☐ ......ike	☐ ......ango
☐ ...... cho	☐ ......ierra
☐ ..... omeo	☐ ......otel
☐ ......lpha	☐ ......ovember
☐ ......ravo	☐ ......oxtrot
☐ ......elta	

4 Make questions and short answers.

1 Mrs Brett / reservation / by email? (No)
   Did Mrs Brett make a reservation by email?
   No, she didn't.

2 Mrs Brett / leave / contact number? (Yes)
   ....
   ....

3 Mrs Brett / reserve / single room? (No)
   ....
   ....

4 the Ronaldos / order / breakfast for two? (Yes)
   ....
   ....

5 they / book / table for 12.30? (No)
   ....
   ....

6 Valerie / offer / a discount? (Yes)
   ....
   ....

5 Rewrite the sentences in the negative.

1 They arrived last night.
   They didn't arrive last night.

2 He confirmed his reservation in writing.
   ....

3 Reception gave room 501 the message.
   ....

4 Room 222 paid their bill last night.
   ....

5 The hotel included breakfast in the special offer.
   ....

6 She spoke to the duty manager.
   ....

7 The head chef made all the main courses and desserts.
   ....

8 He reserved a parking space with his booking.
   ....

6 Use the table to calculate the answers to the questions.

room type	Tariff per room per night			
	1 night	*Sat/Sun (2 nights)*	*3–6 nights*	*7 nights +*
Double	€100	€160	€80	€70
Family	€130	€200	€90	€80
Single	€80	€130	€70	€65
Suite	€180	€280	€150	€140

How much is ...

1 a single room for 3 nights? *€210*
2 a double room for Monday and Tuesday night? ....
3 a suite for Saturday and Sunday night? ....
4 a family room for 10 nights? ....
5 a suite for 3 nights? ....
6 a double room for Friday to Sunday night? ....
7 a single room for 1 night? ....
8 a family room for Saturday to Monday night? ....

7 Find ten more telephone terms in the puzzle. You can read some from left to right (→), some from top to bottom (→), and some diagonally (↗).

```
B A T T E R Y H X S B X N
X I M X R A N A W X U I U
A X D R X I P N X U S R M
V I U X Y E X D A X Y E B
X B M E X T A S X I T C E
Y O K X R X P E S M O H R
I N T E R N A T I O N A L
C A L L V X Y U P B E R X
X F R X H O P Y R I X G E
B X J L S X H F A L D E X
W H E X H L O X T E D X O
D I A L L I N G T O N E L
X P R A X T E C C X I A N
```

1 Look at the pictures and complete the sentences about Bruno's bad day.

1 When Bruno arrived at work this morning he fell on the slippery __floor__ and hurt his ....

2 He picked up a .... bag of potatoes and strained his ....

3 He took salt from the .... and found it was caustic soda.

4 He .... his .... on the food slicer.

5 He ran for the .... when the .... went off, and fell over some boxes.

6 He .... in the restaurant and injured his ....

7 He got a nasty electric .... from a faulty .... Poor old Bruno went home!

2 Match the health and safety regulations a–g with the pictures in exercise 1.

a [2] When lifting heavy objects, bend your knees and don't strain your back.

b [ ] Always put the guard in place before using the food slicer.

c [ ] Clean kitchen floors regularly.

d [ ] Replace damaged carpets.

e [ ] Keep fire exits clear at all times.

f [ ] Replace old and faulty equipment.

g [ ] Don't store cleaning products with food.

3 Complete the table of adjectives and adverbs.

	Adjectives	Adverbs
1	careful	*carefully*
2		clearly
3		early
4	fast	
5		freshly
6	good	
7		hard
8	immediate	
9		late
10	patient	
11		politely
12	quick	
13		quietly
14	regular	
15		seriously
16	slow	

4 Correct the mistakes in the sentences.

1 Please close your door ~~quiet~~ late at night.
.... *quietly* ....

2 Room 356 would like their bill immediate.
....

3 The chef makes freshly bread every morning.
....

4 The staff work very hardly in the busy season.
....

5 The Coral Beach is a well hotel.
....

6 Bruno works very fastly in the kitchen.
....

7 Staff must speak polite to guests.
....

8 Jo was very patiently with the elderly guests.
....

9 He checked the guest list careful.
....

10 The fire alarms are tested regular.
....

5 Rewrite the sentences using adverbs.

1 Stefano is a very quick worker.
Stefano works very quickly.

2 He's a good cook.
....

3 She's a careful driver.
....

4 He's a slow worker.
....

5 We have a regular test drill.
....

6 He gave a serious talk about health and safety.
....

7 Reception staff always give polite answers to guests.
....

8 The cashier asked the man for immediate payment.
....

6 Use the clues to find a useful person in an emergency.

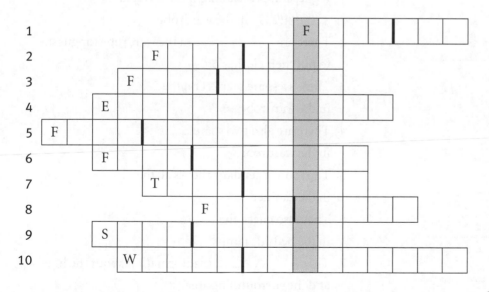

1 You need this to break down a door in a fire. (4,3)
2 The way out in an emergency. (4,4)
3 Leave the building when you hear this. (4,5)
4 A fire .... is useful equipment for a small fire. (12)
5 You can cover a fire with this. (4,7)
6 The chief and his team. (4,7)
7 A practice for an emergency. (4,5)
8 Hotels must have these doors. (4,5)
9 A useful bucket for kitchen fires. (4,6)
10 A fire-fighting shower. (5,9)

20 Giving directions indoors

1 Read the text and answer the questions.

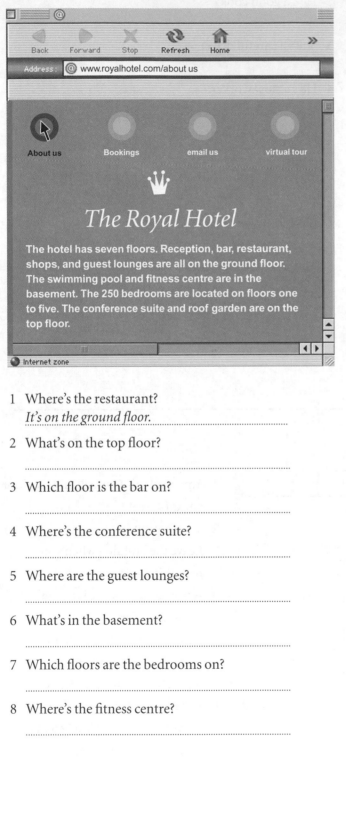

1 Where's the restaurant?
It's on the ground floor.

2 What's on the top floor?

3 Which floor is the bar on?

4 Where's the conference suite?

5 Where are the guest lounges?

6 What's in the basement?

7 Which floors are the bedrooms on?

8 Where's the fitness centre?

2 Read the directions and underline the correct word or phrase in italics.

- Take the lift *to* / *for*[1] the top floor. *Walk* / *Turn*[2] right out of the lift and the conference suite is *on* / *in*[3] your right.
- Go *across* / *down*[4] the lobby. Go *under* / *through*[5] the door. *Take* / *Turn*[6] left and go *up* / *down*[7] the stairs to the basement.
- It's *in* / *on*[8] the ground floor *opposite* / *inside*[9] the lift.
- *Take* / *Go*[10] the lift to the fourth floor. When you *go into* / *come out of*[11] the lift, *turn* / *take*[12] right and room 420 is *at* / *on*[13] your left.
- Walk *past* / *along*[14] the corridor, turn right *at the end* / *at the top*[15] of the corridor. Go *across* / *past*[16] the stairs and the lifts are in front of you.

3 Complete the sentences with the correct item.

light bulbs	drawers	hangers
bedding	welcome folder	trouser press
shaver point	pillows	shelf

1 If guests are cold at night there is spare ....*bedding*.......... in the wardrobe.

2 There are .... in the wardrobe for guests to put their clothes on.

3 There's a spare blanket on the .... in the wardrobe.

4 There are also two spare .... in the wardrobe.

5 The room attendant checks all the .... in the cabinet.

6 They also check the .... in the bedside lamps.

7 The .... has information about the hotel and the surrounding area.

8 Some rooms have a .... for guests' trousers.

9 There's a .... in the bathroom for electric shavers.

4 Look at the pictures of Lyn and Petra checking the room and complete the sentences.

1 Lyn is checking the ...._hangers_........ in the wardrobe.

2 Petra is checking the .... in the bedside lamps.

5 Lyn is checking the welcome ....

6 Petra is checking the ....

9 For the turn-down service, Petra is folding back the ....

10 Lyn is closing the ....

3 Petra is checking the spare bedding on the wardrobe ....

4 Lyn is looking in the .... of the cabinet.

7 Petra is setting the ....

8 Lyn is polishing the ....

5 Complete the crossword using the clues below.

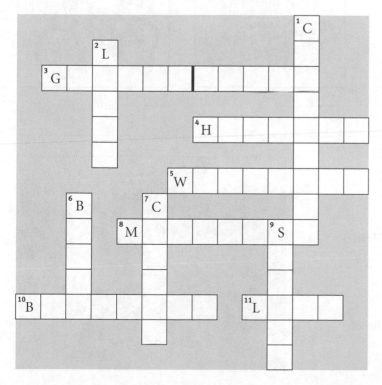

ACROSS

3 Hotel reception is on the
.... (6,5)

4 This is essential in winter. (7)

5 A tall cupboard for clothes. (8)

8 The soft part of the bed. (8)

10 This floor is under the ground floor. (8)

11 Go up or down in this. (4)

DOWN

1 Walk along these to the rooms (9)

2 Guests check in at reception in the
.... (5)

6 The room attendants check all the light
.... (5)

7 A floor-covering. (6)

9 Walk up and down these. (6)

1 Use each word once to complete the text.

theatres	*travel*	gallery
underground	railway station	bus station
cinema	museums	outside

getting around

To ....*travel*........ [1] around the city and to visit places .... [2] the city, you can take a bus from the .... [3]. The .... [4] is really quick for city centre travel. The .... [5] has trains to all parts of the country as well as international services. In the evenings you can see the latest films at the .... [6], and if you prefer a play or a show there are three or four .... [7]. There are a lot of interesting .... [8] which explain our history, and if you like art there is a wonderful .... [9] which has pictures by Matisse, Picasso, and the French impressionists.

2 Look at the pictures and write the different ways you can travel.

...........*by taxi*...........

....

....

....

....

....

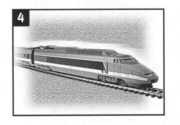

....

....

3 Underline the correct prepositions.

1 Take the bridge <u>over</u> / across the motorway.
2 You can park directly *inside* / *outside* the hotel.
3 Get *on* / *in* the train at Kings Cross and get *to* / *off* at Waverley.
4 Don't turn left or right. Go *straight on* / *right on*.
5 Walk down the street *next to* / *towards* the museum.
6 Go *up* / *along* the hill and turn right at the top.
7 The cinema is just *across* / *opposite* the road from the hotel.
8 The bus station is *in* / *on* the other side of the square.

4 Use the underground map to give the directions.

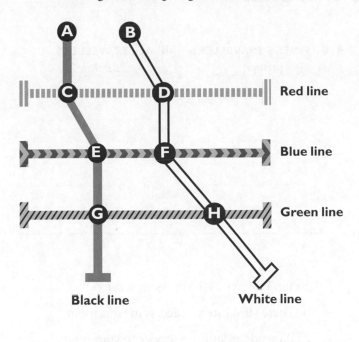

Red line
Blue line
Green line
Black line   **White line**

1 Excuse me. How do I get from A to F?
   Take the Black line two stops south to E.
   Change onto the Blue line and go one stop east.

2 Excuse me. How do I get from B to G?
   ....
   ....

3 Excuse me. How do I get from C to H?
   ....

4 Excuse me. How do I get from A to B?
   ....

5 Excuse me. How do I get from H to A?
   ....
   ....

5 Read sentences 1–8. Then underline true or false for the town or city where you are studying.

1 There's an underground train system.   true/false
2 There's a square outside the busiest railway station.   true/false
3 There's a theatre near your school or college.   true/false
4 The largest hotel is in the centre.   true/false
5 There's a river, and at least one bridge you can go over on foot.   true/false
6 There are more than five museums.   true/false
7 The quickest way to get to the airport is by taxi.   true/false
8 The cheapest way to get to the next big city or town is by bus.   true/false

6 Find nine more London tube stations in the puzzle. You can read some from left to right (→), some from top to bottom (↓), and some diagonally (↗).

```
K X A B O N D S T R E E T X
N I R V X S S M I U T R O V
I N O L G O T X E W Q U T O
G B I N R X S S A T U M O X
H P I C C A D I L L Y A N F
T K I X C I R C U S D R I O
S L A S X O R A B M X B O R
B X Y I T I X Y O L P L X D
R A M C X O B A K E R E U C
I X I P P S T R E E T A X I
D V X R O T X A T R X R E R
G G R E E N P A R K A C X C
E M A X D O W X L A R H F U
C A N A R Y W H A R F X U S
```

22 Facilities for the business traveller

1 Make two lists of the services and facilities for
A (Business travellers), and B (All travellers).

printer	satellite TV	room service
fax	babysitting	pay-per-view films
email	photocopier	video conferencing
broadband	swimming pool	multi-line phones
laundry	car hire	

A BUSINESS TRAVELLERS
printer

....

....

....

....

....

....

B ALL TRAVELLERS
satellite TV

....

....

....

....

....

....

2 Match requests 1–8 and offers a–h.

1 [c] I'd like some shirts washed.

2 [   ] I want to send a fax.

3 [   ] I need to make a copy of a document.

4 [   ] We'd like our children looked after this evening.

5 [   ] I need to print out some documents from my laptop.

6 [   ] Where can I get Internet access?

7 [   ] Can I get something to eat in the middle of the night?

8 [   ] I need to check my email quickly.

a Yes. We have 24-hour room service.

b There's TV Internet access in your room.

c I'll send the laundry service to your room.

d The photocopier is in the business centre on the ground floor.

e I'll ask our babysitting service to contact you.

f The fax machine is in the business centre behind reception.

g Come and use broadband in the business centre.

h There's a printer in our business centre.

3 Use each word once to label the equipment.

| printer |
| digital projector |
| laptop |
| screen |
| microphone |
| photocopier |
| *flip chart* |
| TV/monitor |

flip chart

....

4 Match the phrases to make sentences.

1 | c | The hotel is fully booked at the weekend so
2 | | The fire alarm went off at 7 a.m. but
3 | | The conference delegates arrive at 6 p.m. so
4 | | Both the fitness centre
5 | | They wanted to book the meeting rooms but
6 | | You can send emails from your room but
7 | | Both the large meeting room
8 | | The customer requested information about our conference centre

a it was only a test drill.

b the printer and copier are in the business centre.

c we can't take any more bookings.

d everything must be ready by then.

e they didn't want accommodation.

f so we sent her an information pack.

g and the swimming pool close at 10 p.m.

h and the banqueting room hold 500 people.

---

5 Underline the correct words in italics to complete the email.

File   Edit   View   Insert   Format   Tools   Actions   Help

Dear Sir/Madam

My *work / company*[1] is *doing / planning*[2] a three-day *conference / meeting*[3] in Prague next September.

We *want / require*[4] meeting rooms and *single / one*[5] room accommodation for all *candidates / delegates*[6].

Please *advise / tell*[7] me re the availability of dates and send me your *conference / meeting*[8] information pack.

Regards

A Dobbs

Conference organizer

6 Use the clues to find an important business presentation facility.

1 You use this to put information onto a large screen. (9)

2 You can make copies of paper documents with this machine. (11)

3 What does *www* stand for? (5,4,3)

4 Messages that are sent via the Internet. (6)

5 High-speed data lines use .... connections. (9)

6 To print out a document you need a .... (7)

7 Face-to-face meeting via the Internet. (5,10)

8 We access the World Wide Web via the .... (8)

9 Printers, copiers, and fax machines are in the hotel .... centre. (8)

10 You can find information about the hotel on its .... (7)

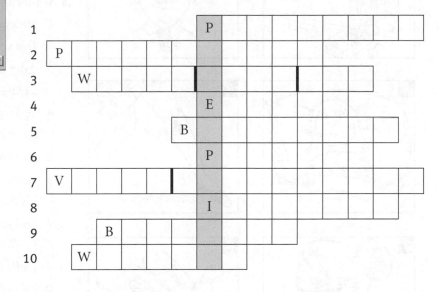

23 Offering help and advice

1 Match the sentences with the pictures.

a [2] The little boy has earache.

b [ ] The kitchen porter has cut his finger on a knife.

c [ ] The room attendant has hurt her ankle
on the stairs.

d [ ] The man has a bad stomach ache.

e [ ] The girl has a temperature.

f [ ] Joanne has filled in an accident report form.

g [ ] The woman has injured her leg.

h [ ] The first aider has put a plaster on the cut.

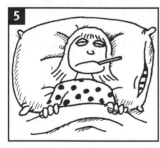

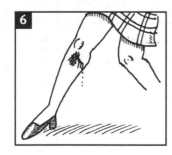

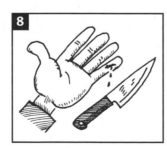

2 Complete the sentences with the Present
Perfect tense of the verbs in brackets.
Use short forms if appropriate.

1 The group from Japan ....*have*........ just
........*arrived*........ . (arrive)

2 Lyn and Petra .... just ....
servicing the rooms. (finish)

3 The chef .... here for about
ten years. (work)

4 I .... in the city all my life. (live)

5 The group from Germany ....
.... yet. (not check in)

6 .... anybody .... my pen? (see)

7 The guest in room 442 ....
his bill yet. (not pay)

8 Mr Lee from 209 .... just ....
the stairs! (fall down)

9 The new guests ....
their passports to reception yet. (not give)

10 She .... just .... her hand
on the slicer! (cut)

3 Underline the correct form of the verb.

1 He *started* / *has started* work at ten o'clock.

2 *Did you eat* / *Have you eaten* anything yet today?

3 After he fainted, she *gave* / *has given* him
a glass of water.

4 Yesterday one of the kitchen porters *cut* / *has cut* his
hand badly.

5 Last week he *burnt* / *has burnt* his arm on the hob.

6 Mary, come quickly! Mr Becks *fell* / *has fallen* over in
his room.

7 *Did you call* / *Have you called* an ambulance yet?

8 I *called* / *have called* a doctor five minutes ago.

9 I *fell* / *have fallen* off my bike on Tuesday.

10 I *didn't see* / *haven't seen* the nurse yet.

4 Match sentences 1–8 with the advice in a–h.

1 [b] I think I have flu. I feel terrible.

2 [ ] Someone has stolen my handbag.

3 [ ] There's smoke coming out of that building.

4 [ ] He has really bad toothache.

5 [ ] Do you think it's going to rain?

6 [ ] I feel faint.

7 [ ] I was late for work today.

8 [ ] What can I give my mother for her birthday?

a We should call the fire brigade. It looks serious.

b You should spend the day in bed.

c You should buy her some flowers.

d He should see a dentist.

e You should go to the police station.

f You should arrive on time tomorrow.

g You should sit down for a minute.

h Yes, I do. You should take an umbrella.

5 Put the sentences in the dialogue in the correct order.

a [ ] CHEF: One of the waitresses has burnt her hand on the coffee machine.

b [ ] MARY: Yes. I'll get my first aid kit.

c [ ] CHEF: Yes, of course. I've just come off duty so I have time to take her.

d [ ] MARY: Let me look at it first. Can you take her to the hospital if it's a bad burn?

e [1] CHEF: Mary, you're the first aider. We need you in the kitchen.

f [ ] MARY: Right. Tell her to put her hand in cold water.

g [ ] CHEF: Do you think she needs a doctor?

h [ ] MARY: Why? What's happened?

i [ ] CHEF: OK. I'll tell her. Can you come now?

6 Complete the crossword using the clues below.

ACROSS

2 You often get this common illness in winter. (1, 4)

4 With this illness you feel hot, cold, and full of aches and pains. (3)

6 This person looks after you in hospital. (5)

7 A pain in one of your teeth. (9)

8 A pain in your head. (8)

10 If you have a health problem, you need to see this person. (6)

11 Heat, illness, or pain may make you do this. (5)

DOWN

1 You get a .... when you touch something very hot. (4)

3 With this illness you need to visit the toilet regularly. (9)

5 A common illness where breathing is difficult. (6)

9 This person checks your teeth. (7)

Dealing with problems

1 Complete the sentences with the correct form of the verb.

1 The floor in room 452 _hasn't been cleaned_ .
   a isn't cleaned   b hasn't clean   c *hasn't been cleaned*

2 The bed ....
   a isn't done   b hasn't been made c hasn't made

3 The towels ....
   a haven't been changed b haven't changed c aren't changed

4 Room 261's shirts .... yet from the laundry.
   a hasn't arrived back   b haven't arrived back c aren't arrived back

5 The shower ....
   a haven't been fixed   b hasn't fixed   c hasn't been fixed

6 The bedside lamp bulbs ....
   a hasn't replaced   b haven't been replaced c hasn't been replaced

7 The air-conditioning in room 306 ....
   a hasn't been fixed   b hasn't fixed   c haven't fixed

8 The waste bin ....
   a isn't emptied   b hasn't emptied c hasn't been emptied

2 Write which member of staff is responsible for solving problems 1–9.

room attendant
porter
maintenance man
housekeeper
service engineer

maintenance man

3 Rewrite the sentences in the Passive.

1 The room attendant should have cleaned the room.   *The room should have been cleaned this morning.*

2 The porter should have taken up the luggage. ....

3 The receptionist should have passed on the message. ....

4 The laundry should have sent back the shirts. ....

5 Maintenance should have fixed the shower. ....

6 Housekeeping should have replaced the toiletries. ....

7 The service engineer should have repaired the TV. ....

8 Reception should have given him a non-smoking room. ....

---

4 Match problems 1–8 with solutions a–h.

1 | *b* | My room smells of smoke.

2 | | I can't sleep with the traffic noise.

3 | | My room hasn't been serviced today.

4 | | I didn't receive my wake-up call.

5 | | The toilet in our bathroom is blocked.

6 | | Our wet towels haven't been changed.

7 | | Our luggage hasn't arrived in our room yet.

8 | | The bedside lights aren't working.

a I'll ask the porter to bring it up straightaway.

b I'll move you to a non-smoking room immediately.

c I'll ask housekeeping to bring you some fresh ones.

d I'm sorry. I'll look into it for you.

e Would you like to move to a quieter room at the back of the hotel?

f I'll send someone up with new light bulbs.

g I'll ask the maintenance man to come up straightaway.

h I'll inform housekeeping and ask them to attend to it immediately.

---

5 Find nine more items usually found in hotel rooms in the puzzle. You can read some from left to right (→), some from top to bottom (↑), and some diagonally (↗).

```
T R O U S E R P R E S S X R T
X M A E R X S I B E X O S U X
F L O W E R S X U D O N X O A
R E X L Y O R S X A V E N O C
U T R E X T S C R E X E N D E
I W R I T I N G P A P E R A X
T X L I T I X A P X W I S O L
B R U X I N C X K L L X E N O
O X I V Z R X R E Q U O W I X
W E N V E L O P E S X N I D H
L O N W X D F X E K L X N E E
P X O D T E X Y L J E S G N X
S H O E C L E A N I N G K I T
S T X L A N C X T E B X I T E
Z E B R X N B Y D X S T T E X
```

PLEASE DO NOT DISTURB

25 Paying bills

1 Use each phrase once to complete the sentences.

cash	receipt
Visa	*payment*
credit card	VAT
debit card	company
vouchers	Mastercard
traveller's cheques	

1 Most hotels accept ....*payment*.... by credit card.

2 .... customers have up to fifty days to pay their card company.

3 .... payments are taken directly from the customer's bank account.

4 .... and .... are two of the most widely-used credit cards.

5 People don't usually carry large amounts of .... on holiday.

6 .... can soon be replaced if they are lost or stolen.

7 In business travel, the .... usually pays for the room and meals.

8 Business travellers need a .... for their accounts department.

9 .... is usually included in hotel bills.

10 Travellers sometimes have pre-paid .... for their accommodation.

2 Underline the correct form of the verb.

1 Mary <u>works</u> / *is working* as a receptionist. At the moment she *checks in* / <u>*is checking in*</u> some new guests.

2 Mrs de Canio *leaves* / *is leaving* for the airport. She always *pays* / *is paying* her bill by credit card.

3 Business travellers usually *pay* / *are paying* with their company credit card.

4 The bus for the airport *leaves* / *is leaving* every 20 minutes.

5 The chef *prepares* / *is preparing* the main courses for today's lunch. The sous chef *helps* / *is helping* him.

6 The German group *leaves* / *is leaving* now. Guests usually *check out* / *are checking out* before 10 a.m.

7 First, the guest *signs* / *is signing* the Visa slip, and then the cashier *gives* / *is giving* her a copy of the bill.

8 The restaurant *serves* / *is serving* lobster today. They usually *serve* / *are serving* it once a week.

3 Replace the words in italics with object pronouns.

a Sylvie gave ~~the man~~ ......*him*...... [1] his bill and he gave *Sylvie* .... [2] his credit card.
She handed *the man* .... [3] the Visa slip and asked *the man* .... [4] to sign *the slip* .... [5] .
He thanked *Sylvie* .... [6] for an enjoyable stay.

b The kitchen porters peeled the potatoes and put *the potatoes* .... [7] in the saucepan.
Then they filled *the saucepan* .... [8] with water and put *the saucepan* .... [9] on the hob.
Next, the chef asked *the kitchen porters* .... [10] to prepare the green beans.

c The hotel apologized to *my wife and I* .... [11] for the mistake.
They said *the mistake* .... [12] was because of a computer fault.
They gave *my wife and I* .... [13] a bottle of champagne and some flowers and offered *my wife and I* .... [14] a discount on our bill.

4 Write the names of the countries represented in the pictures. Then match them with the currencies.

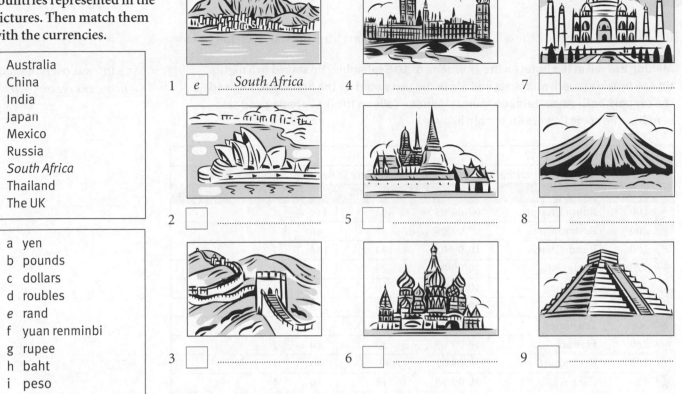

Australia	
China	
India	
Japan	
Mexico	
Russia	
South Africa	
Thailand	
The UK	

1 | e | *South Africa*

2

3

4

5

6

7

8

9

a yen
b pounds
c dollars
d roubles
e rand
f yuan renminbi
g rupee
h baht
i peso

---

5 Put the sentences in the correct order to make a dialogue between a waiter and a customer.

WAITER:

a [1] Here's your bill, sir.

b [ ] Here's your credit card receipt and your VAT receipt. Thank you very much.

c [ ] Yes. The total shows a 10% service charge.

d [ ] Certainly, sir. Could you sign here, please?

e [ ] Yes. Mastercard is fine.

f [ ] Thank you. Good evening. We hope to see you again.

CUSTOMER:

g [ ] Right. Could I have a VAT receipt, please?

h [ ] Thank you very much. We really enjoyed our meal. This is for you.

i [ ] Is service included in the bill?

j [ ] OK. I have a pen, thank you.

k [ ] Thank you. Do you take Mastercard?

6 Use the clues to find the missing form of payment.

1 Another word for a *bill*. (7)

2 Add everything up to get a .... (5)

3 You don't pay more for these items. They are .... in the bill. (8)

4 You get this after you pay a bill. (7)

5 You get this back when you pay more than the exact cash payment. (6)

6 Restaurants often charge 10% or more for this. (7)

7 Items not included in the price. (6)

8 If the bill is ...., it shows every item. (8)

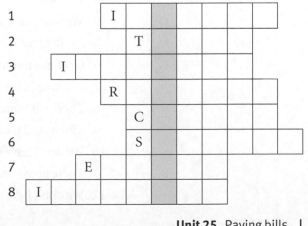

1 Read the text and study the bill. Then find six more items Mr King was overcharged for.

Mr King arrived at the hotel on the afternoon of 10 September. He stayed two nights. He had breakfast both mornings and ate in the restaurant on the first night. He used the car park both days. He made some telephone calls on the first evening and also sent his wife some flowers for her birthday.

Mr King was overcharged for:

1 *Room charge on 09/09*
2 ....
3 ....
4 ....
5 ....
6 ....
7 ....

Billing Mr King Room 207					
Arrival **10/09/05** Departing **12/09/05** Persons **1** Rate Code **RACK** Balance **804.00**					
	Department	Date	Amount	Price	Quantity
100	Room Charge	09/09/05	144	144	1
200	Restaurant	09/09/05	46	46	1
100	Room Charge	10/09/05	144	144	1
120	Breakfast	10/09/05	20	20	1
500	Telephone	10/09/05	10	10	1
500	Telephone	10/09/05	8	8	1
500	Telephone	10/09/05	23	23	1
320	Flowers	10/09/05	30	30	1
200	Restaurant	10/09/05	60	60	1
400	Car park	10/09/05	10	10	1
150	Minibar	10/09/05	18	18	1
100	Room Charge	11/09/05	144	144	1
120	Breakfast	11/09/05	20	20	1
180	Laundry	11/09/05	22	22	1
500	Telephone	11/09/05	15	15	1
400	Car park	11/09/05	10	10	1
200	Restaurant	11/09/05	60	60	1
120	Breakfast	12/09/05	20	20	1

2 Calculate what Mr King's correct bill total should have been.

His correct bill total should have been: ....

3 Find the ten incorrect sentences and correct them using *much*, *many*, or *a lot of*. Tick (✔) the correct sentences.

1 There aren't ~~much~~ people in the restaurant tonight. *many/a lot of*
2 How many is a double room for the weekend? ....
3 We haven't had many guests from the US this year. ....
4 We don't have much rooms left at the weekend. ....
5 Do they need many equipment for the conference? ....
6 Chef has put much pasta dishes on the menu today. ....
7 She takes a lot of money in tips in her job. ....
8 There isn't many wine left in the bottle. ....
9 Much staff take their holidays in low season. ....
10 We don't have much people from South America staying. ....
11 There aren't much different wines on the wine list. ....
12 We don't have many time to service all the rooms. ....

4 Rewrite the two jumbled conversations in the correct order.

Straightaway, sir. Here it is.
No sir, it isn't included.
Could I have my bill, please?
Twenty euros. Thank you very much, sir. Just sign here.
Certainly, madam. I'll just print it out for you.
   How would you like to pay?
Do you take Mastercard?
Actually madam, the room service was for dry cleaning
   and pressing on Tuesday.
I'd like to settle my bill, please. Room 432.
The extras are for the car park, minibar, and room service.
By Visa.
Visa is fine, madam. Here we are. Three nights, accommodation
   with breakfast.
Please add 20 euros to my Mastercard payment.
Yes. Mastercard is fine, sir.
Right. And the extras?
But I didn't use room service.
Oh, yes! I forgot. That's right then.
Is service included in the bill?
OK. Thank you. It was a very good meal.

1 WOMAN: *I'd like to settle my bill, please. Room 432.*
   CASHIER: ....
   WOMAN: ....
   CASHIER: ....
   WOMAN: ....
   CASHIER: ....
   WOMAN: ....
   CASHIER: ....
   WOMAN: ....

2 MAN: *Could I have my bill, please?*
   WAITER: ....
   MAN: ....
   WAITER: ....
   MAN: ....
   WAITER: ....
   MAN: ....
   WAITER: ....
   MAN: ....

5 Complete the crossword using the clues below.

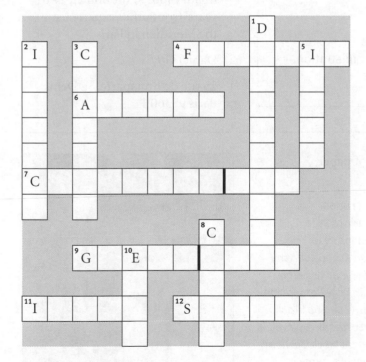

ACROSS

4 The .... system processes guests. (7)
6 When you click on a name, the bill will ....
   on screen. (6)
7 Reception is busy with this in the morning. (8, 3)
9 Fidelio's record of guests is the ....
   .... (5, 4)
11 *Room charge*, *breakfast*, and *laundry* are all
   .... on the bill. (5)
12 Just click to change computer .... (6)

DOWN

1 To see who's checking out, click on .... (10)
2 Another word for *bill*. (7)
3 The bill shows the .... for all the items. (7)
5 When the payment is processed, the computer will
   .... an invoice. (5)
8 .... on icons with the mouse. (5)
10 The opposite of *difficult*. (4)

27 Applying for a job

1 Complete the CV using the information on the right.

CURRICULUM VITAE

1	Surname	*Dupont*
2	First names	
3	Address	
4	Telephone number	
5	Mobile number	
6	email address	
7	Date of birth	

	Education	• Lycée St. Denis • School of Business Administration, Clichy
8	Qualifications	• •
9	Work experience	• •
	Skills	Word processing, bookkeeping, intermediate English language
10	Personal qualities	
	References	• The Principal, Lycée St. Denis • Head of Dept of Business Administration, Clichy College

a +33 141 35 67 90

b 23 August 1985

c *Dupont*

d danieldupont@yahoo.com

e Baccalaureate Professionale; BEP certificate in Tourism and Hospitality

f Hardworking, well organized, sociable, and friendly

g +33 77973846392

h Porter and doorman student holiday jobs at the Sofitel; Two years' front office experience at the Meridien in Paris

i Daniel Guy

j 25 rue de Bonaparte, St. Denis, Paris 95360 1

---

2 Use the information below to write Ulrika's CV on a piece of paper, or in your notebook.

My name's Ulrika Mansky. I live in Düsseldorf at 18 Mozartstrasse. I'm 19 years old. My date of birth is 3 April 1986. My email address is umansky@wanadoo.com and my mobile phone number in Germany is +49 7631 24 38 65. I attended high school in Düsseldorf until I passed my international baccalaureate in 2004. I've just finished a one-year training course in tourism and hospitality and now I have a diploma in hotel reception work. My word processing skills are excellent and I'm familiar with the Fidelio and Galileo systems. I speak and write English at a good intermediate level. I've worked for the last three summers at the family-run Mozarts Hotel near my home. I've worked on reception and as a waitress. The owner's name is Frau Margrit Becker. I'm friendly and hard-working. I like responsibility.

3 Answer the questions about writing letters.

1 How would you begin a letter to a woman whose name you don't know?
Dear ......Madam......

2 How would you end it?
....

3 How would you begin a letter to a Mr Pons?
Dear ....

4 How would you end it?
....

5 How would you begin a letter to Mr Pons' wife?
Dear ....

6 How would you begin a letter to their daughter? You don't know if she is married or single.
Dear ....

7 How would you begin a letter asking for a job application form? You don't know the name of the person responsible.
Dear ....

8 How would you ask for confirmation of a reservation in writing?
Would you .... ?

9 How would you begin a letter responding to a job advertisement?
With ....

10 How would you begin a letter applying for a job?
I would ....

---

4 Complete the covering letter using the notes below.

Had three years' experience under a great chef. Learnt a lot. Now looking for new challenges, new menus. Hardworking professional. Like responsibility. Good teamworker. Have always been interested in travel and other countries. Would be good to have the opportunity of using and improving English language skills. Clean driving licence.

Dear Sir/Madam

RE: JOB APPLICATION FOR SOUS CHEF

I enclose my completed application form for the post of sous chef at your hotel in Ireland. I am currently working at the Metropole as a commis chef under Monsieur Blanc.

He is a ....great chef........ [1] and I have ....[2] working under him. I now feel it is time to look for

...............................[3] and to master ....[4].

I am a ....[5] and would enjoy the

...............................[6] that your post offers. I have always been

interested in ....[7], and this would also be a good

opportunity to ....[8] and ....[9] my

language skills. I have had a clean ....[10] for three

years.

I look forward to hearing from you.

Yours faithfully

5 Find ten more job application words in the puzzle. You can read some from left to right (→), some from top to bottom (↑), and some diagonally (↗).

```
R E S P O N S I B I L I T Y
E X M H A R D W O R K I N G
F R A X O L X O L Y M O X S
E A X S L X T O L X I E R O
R Y T I X C W U X T M V A C
E X K O L G X E A B U X S I
N S X U S X O C F A J Z X A
C E X P E R I E N C E X Y B
E A T T X F R I E N D L Y L
D R I V I N G L I C E N C E
X I N L X H A E F E X L T O
N X A R U O G H X N V O U X
P U X O R G A N I Z E D X Y
Q U I K X C H A L L E N G E
```

28 The interview

1 Make two lists of the words and phrases, matching the opposites.

> smile not well-informed relaxed
>
> look unhappy positive attitude
>
> tense speak clearly nervous
>
> smart *don't concentrate*
>
> confident well-prepared
>
> avoid eye contact
>
> speak quietly well-informed
>
> *listen* badly dressed
>
> negative attitude
>
> unprepared make eye contact

Good interview techniques	How NOT to be
listen	*don't concentrate*

2 Complete the letter with the verbs in brackets in the correct future form: Present Simple, -*ing*, *going to*, or *will*. Use short forms if appropriate.

> Dear Markus
>
> How are you?
>
> I ____*finish*____[1] (finish) college next month.
> First, I _____[2] (have) a holiday, then
> I _____[3] (look for) a job. My sister and
> I _____[4] (visit) our grandparents in Italy. We
> _____[5] (return) on 31 August and
> I _____[6] (have to) find a job.
> I _____[7] (go) to our local employment office
> and I _____[8] (check) all the internet job sites.
> I hope I _____[9] (find) something in one of the
> big hotels. After I find a job, I _____[10]
> (look for) an apartment near my work.
>
> What _____ you _____[11] (do) in
> September? _____ you _____[12]
> (come) to France? I _____[13] (send) you my
> new address and you can visit me.
>
> Best wishes
>
> *Toni*

---

3 Use each word once to complete the job interview.

> stayed   leave
> spend   hotel chain
> taught   study
> useful   *old*
> moved   staff
> all over improve
> course   push
> found   skills
> taking   joining
> dealing   opportunities

INTERVIEWER: So, Carmen, would you like to tell me something about yourself?

CARMEN: Yes, of course. I'm 22 years ____*old*____[1]. I was born in Pamplona and _____[2] to Madrid four years ago to do a _____[3] at the tourism college.

INTERVIEWER: What course did you take?

CARMEN: I took a two year course in tourism and hotel management and got my reception manager's diploma.

INTERVIEWER: Did you _____[4] English on the course?

CARMEN: Oh, yes. We had four lessons a week with our English teacher. She _____[5] us a lot of _____[6] language for _____[7] reservations on the phone and _____[8] with guests at reception, as well as emails.

INTERVIEWER: So, what did you do after college?

CARMEN: My first job was in a small family-run hotel in Pamplona.

INTERVIEWER: I see you only ....⁹ there six months. Why did you ....¹⁰?

CARMEN: Well, to be honest, I felt I wasn't using my ....¹¹. I felt I needed to give my career a ....¹² or I wouldn't get much experience in large hotels.

INTERVIEWER: So you ....¹³ a job at the Ramada here in Barcelona.

CARMEN: Yes. I thought that by ....¹⁴ a big ....¹⁵ like Ramada there would be a lot more ....¹⁶ for me in terms of work and travel.

INTERVIEWER: Well, you're right. We do have opportunities for bright young ....¹⁷ in our sister hotels ....¹⁸ the world. Where are you hoping to travel?

CARMEN: First, I would like to ....¹⁹ at least two years in the UK to ....²⁰ my English, and after that maybe South America …

---

4 Read the text about the family and answer the questions.

My aunt Vivienne is married to Henry. Her parents-in-law live in Switzerland near her brother, Robert. Uncle Robert has two sons, Charles and Peter. Charles and Peter have just one cousin, Charlotte (that's me). Last summer I visited my uncle Henry's parents and met Charles, Peter, and their stepsister, Karen. Next year we're all going to stay with aunt Vivienne in Brittany. She loves it when her nephews and nieces come to stay.

1 Who is aunt Vivienne's husband?
   Henry

2 Where do aunt Vivienne's in-laws live? ....

3 Who is uncle Robert?
   ....

4 Who are Karen's stepbrothers?
   ....

5 What relation are Charles, Peter, and Karen to Charlotte?
   ....

6 What relation are they to aunt Vivienne? ....

5 Use the clues to find one of Jamie Oliver's personal qualities.

1 Another word for your *working life*. (6)

2 *I was pleased to be a* .... *for a second interview.* (9)

3 *The personnel officer made a* .... *of candidates.* (9)

4 Jamie Oliver is famous. He has made several of these. (2,6)

5 Interviewers always ask about your previous job .... (10)

6 If you work well in a team, you're a good .... (10)

7 Several hotels in the same management group are called a .... (5,5)

8 With a well-written CV, you have a good chance of an .... (9)

9 Jamie Oliver studied for his chef's .... in London. (11)

1		C							

2	C							

3					S						

4				T					

5			E					

6			T					

7			H						

8	I						

9	C							

Answer key

Unit 1

1
1 parking space   2 double room
3 message   4 computer screen
5 printer   6 reserve
7 keyboard   8 connect
9 credit card   10 reception
11 number

missing word: reservation

2
2 reserve/book   3 speak   4 connect
5 take   6 make   7 tell
8 book/reserve 9 have

3
2 Could I   3 I'd like   4 Could I
5 Can I   6 I'd like   7 Could I
8 I'd like   9 I'd like   10 Could I

4
2 e   3 h   4 b   5 g
6 a   7 d   8 f

5
2 Good morning, Dr Obeda.
3 Good afternoon, Mrs Obeda.
4 Good evening, Dr Obeda.
5 Good evening, Miss Obeda.
6 Goodnight.   7 Goodbye.

Unit 2

1
car park   exchange bureau
Internet access   air-conditioning
international cuisine   swimming pool
cocktail bar   satellite TV
à la carte menu   information desk
disabled facilities   cloakroom

2
2 true   3 true   4 false   5 true
6 false   7 true   8 false

3
2 there are   3 there are   4 Is there
5 there's   6 Is there   7 there is
8 are there   9 there are

4
2 g   3 a   4 b   5 h   6 i
7 f   8 j   9 c   10 d

5
2 in   3 is   4 There   5 's
6 bar   7 menu   8 cuisine   9 are   10 car park

6
thirty 30   thirteen 13   fourteen 14
forty 40   twelve 12   twenty 20
fifteen 15   fifty 50   eighty 80
eighteen 18   two hundred 200
seventeen 17   seventy 70   sixteen 16
sixty 60   ninety 90   nineteen 19

Unit 3

1
2 sauna   3 guest   4 departure
5 reservation 6 September   7 tonight
8 arrive

2
2 Do, don't   3 Does, doesn't 4 Does, does
5 Do, don't   6 Do, do

3
2 Do you have a double room for Saturday night?
3 Do you have a parking space?
4 Does the bathroom have a shower and a bath?
5 Do you have a twin room for tonight?
6 Does the hotel have a swimming pool?
7 Does the hotel have an exchange bureau?
8 Does the hotel have a garden?

4
2 to   3 at   4 from   5 to
6 In   7 at   8 at   9 In
10 in   11 at   12 on   13 In
14 from   15 to   16 on

5
Dear Mrs Fong
Regarding your request for six double
rooms in August.
Please confirm in writing with dates
as soon as possible.
Regards
Roberto Gil
Reservations Manager
Telephone: 0034 193 762 51

6

```
X A H X R T X I R X
P X U S S X R E N Y
A P S X T T H U X T
X O B R O T H E R I
U M A X O G A F X R
X O N M V Z R A E X
J O D A U G H T E R
S D X T W I S H X U
F X S H W I F E Y T
X C C O S X I R I X
```

(BROTHER, DAUGHTER, WIFE, HUSBAND, MOTHER, FATHER, SON diagonals highlighted)

Unit 4

1
2 e   3 g   4 f   5 h   6 a   7 b   8 d

2
2 When does the restaurant open?
It opens from Tuesday to Sunday.
3 What time does the restaurant open for lunch?
It opens at 12.00.
4 What time does Steve start work?
He starts work at 10.30.
5 When does the restaurant close?
It closes at midnight.
6 When do the waiters finish work?
They finish work at two in the morning.

3
2 on the 25th of June   3 on the 28th of June
4 on the 9th of July   5 on the 16th of July
6 on the 18th of July   7 on the 20th of July
8 on Friday the 24th of July

4
1 March   2 Saturday   3 November
4 December   5 Wednesday   6 April
7 July   8 Tuesday   9 Thursday
10 Friday   11 October   12 January

missing word: cancellation

5
2 rarely   3 never
4 always   5 often
6 rarely   7 sometimes, sometimes
8 always   9 often

6
2 never   3 holiday   4 opens
5 fully booked   6 customer   7 serve
8 cancellation   9 family   10 reservation

Unit 5

1
2 d   3 e   4 a   5 b   6 h   7 c   8 f

2
2 d   I'm afraid Nadine's on holiday.
3 g   I'm sorry, the manager's in a meeting.
4 c   I'm sorry, we're fully booked tonight.
5 f   Unfortunately, the restaurant closes at 9.00.
6 e   I'm afraid the car park's full today.
7 b   I'm afraid the swimming pool closes at 10.00.

3
2 we're   3 she's   4 they're
5 he isn't   6 you aren't   7 here's
8 there's   9 there isn't   10 there aren't
11 we can't   12 I can't   13 they don't
14 he doesn't   15 we don't

4
2 doesn't   3 don't   4 can
5 isn't   6 're   7 can't
8 aren't

5
2 c   3 b   4 a   5 f   6 e

6
Across
1 mobile phone   3 lunch
5 unable to   6 accept
7 weekend   9 single room
10 answer   11 bath
12 anything

Down
1 mid-afternoon   2 refuse
4 closed   6 adjoining
8 regret

Unit 6

1
2 i   3 g   4 a/e   5 h
6 a/e   7 c   8 f   9 b

2
2 your   3 her   4 their   5 Their
6 His   7 your   8 Your   9 my
10 my/our 11 our

3
2 a   3 f   4 d   5 b
6 h   7 g   8 c

4
2 name   3 checks
4 registration card   5 fills in
6 receptionist   7 key card
8 porter

5
2 true   3 false   4 false   5 true
6 true   7 true   8 false   9 true
10 false

6

```
X B L U G G A G E E X S
A R R I V E Y K X A S R
R F X I M K C X U E S E
O F D G X E A S R R X S
O I X U H Y X D P X X E
M L A C X C D I A X O R
N L X F I A V X S I M V
U X P R E R X K S M X A
M N X M A D U L P X R T
B P O R T E R X O L T I
E H Y X I K A R R I X O
R E G I S T R A T I O N
```

(LUGGAGE, ARRIVE, ROOM NUMBER, PORTER, REGISTRATION, RESERVATION, KEY CARD highlighted)

Unit 7

1
2 Can I have   3 Shall I
4 Can I have   5 Would you like
6 Could I have   7 Would you like
8 Can we have

2
2 e   3 a   4 g   5 f   6 h   7 c   8 b

3
1 sweet, medium dry, white, red, sparkling
2 large, small, draught, bottled
3 large, small, single, double
4 still, sparkling

4
2 cocktail   3 beer   4 gin
5 wine   6 Bacardi   7 Margarita
8 sparkling

5
2 ice and lemon
3 Fifteen
4 A glass of white wine and a whisky
5 dry or medium dry wine
6 a large or a small whisky
7 Thirteen
8 An apple juice, a mineral water, and a brandy
9 still or sparkling mineral water
10 double or a single brandy
11 Fourteen

6
1 vermouth   2 cocktail   3 orange juice
4 tequila   5 beer   6 vodka
7 ginger ale   8 white wine   9 lemonade
10 tonic   11 sherry

missing word: mineral water

Unit 8

1
2 spoon   3 shaker   4 cubes
5 olive   6 ice   7 lemon
8 sauce   9 sugar

2
2 a   3 f   4 c   5 b   6 e

3
2 Squeeze   3 Strain   4 Fill   5 Add
6 Pour   7 Serve   8 Stir   9 Shake
10 Garnish

4
2 f   3 e   4 a   5 c   6 b   7 d

5
2 Next, add three measures of light rum.
3 Then squeeze the juice of half a lemon.
4 Add the lemon juice and a teaspoon of caster sugar.
5 Next, shake well.
6 Then strain into a cocktail glass.
7 Finally, garnish with a slice of lemon.

6 **Across**
4 crushed ice   6 garnish
7 Cuba Libre   9 bar spoon
10 Manhattan   11 lime juice

Down
1 glass   2 Americano
3 cocktail shaker   5 Margarita
8 bitters

Unit 9

1
2 onion   3 mushroom   4 duck's
5 moules   6 salad

2
2 **d** toast   3 **h** tea
4 **j** egg and bacon   5 **e** salad
6 **g** sandwich   7 **b** soup
8 **e** salad   9 **b** soup
10 **a** steak and chips   11 **f** mussels
12 **i** lamb cutlets

3
2 ✔   3 ✔   4 a table
5 the soup of the day   6 ✔
7 the wine list   8 a pot of tea   9 half a bottle
10 ✔

4 *C*: glass of wine, double whisky, starter, aperitif, bottle of water, cocktail, taxi, parking space
U: water, toast, money, milk, luggage, ice, time, help
C/U: tea, coffee, fish

5
2 Would you like an aperitif?
 Yes, please. A gin and tonic.
3 Can I change some money here?
 Yes. There's an exchange bureau in the lobby.
4 Could we have some mineral water?
 Would you like a large bottle or a small bottle?
5 Could I have a sandwich and an orange juice, please?
 Would you like some ice in your orange juice?
6 Could you call a taxi?
 Certainly.
 Would you like some help with your luggage?

6
2 h   3 c   4 d/f   5 a
6 d/f   7 e   8 b   9 g

7

```
G X O K M X I F P E X S
I I R X I C R X F R U X
X O B M M O N K F I S H
P R X A B O L K X V I N
C X H S M X U L K Z B X
H F I L L E T S T E A K
A P A A X O D X I N C M
L S N M U X A R W I O X
I J X B E E F A S X N U
B E C O X I R X I M E X
U X E B S P X T U X L E
T O M X C H I C K E N O
```

Unit 10

1
2 h   3 g   4 e   5 d
6 c   7 b   8 a

2
2 false   3 false   4 true
5 true   6 false   7 false
8 true   9 true   10 false

3
1 The United States   2 Brazil   3 Morocco
4 Portugal   5 Spain   6 Britain
7 France   8 Germany   9 Italy
10 Japan

4

Country	Nationality	Language
Brazil	*Brazilian*	*Portuguese*
Britain	British	English
France	French	French
Germany	German	German
Italy	*Italian*	Italian
Japan	Japanese	Japanese
Morocco	Moroccan	*Arabic*
Portugal	Portuguese	Portuguese
Spain	Spanish	Spanish
The United States	*American*	English

5
2 some   3 any   4 any   5 some
6 some   7 some   8 any

6
1 blackcurrant   2 Danish blue
3 Manchego   4 vanilla
5 raspberry   6 apple pie
7 Camembert   8 Mozzarella
9 fruit salad   10 ice cream

missing word: chocolate mousse

Unit 11

1
2 g   3 h   4 f   5 c
6 e   7 b   8 a

2
2 Pinot Grigio is a dry white wine.
3 Champagne and Cava are sparkling wines.
4 Riesling is a non-sparkling wine.
5 Port is a fortified wine from Portugal.
6 Merlot is a full-bodied red wine.
7 St. Emilion is a smooth Bordeaux wine.
8 Riesling is a German white wine.

3

Adjective	Comparative
cheap	*cheaper*
expensive	*more expensive*
dry	drier
sweet	sweeter
smooth	smoother
rough	rougher
good	better
bad	worse
full-bodied	more full-bodied
light	lighter
famous	more famous

4
2 Champagne is more famous than Cava and Sekt.
3 Sauvignon Blanc is sweeter than Pinot Grigio.
4 St. Emilion is smoother than a cheap Bordeaux wine.
5 Sauvignon Blanc is drier than Chardonnay.
6 Chardonnay is not as light as Frascati.
7 Other sparkling wines are not as expensive as Champagne.
8 A Bordeaux wine is more full-bodied than a young Beaujolais.
9 A good claret is better than a cheap red wine.

5 Model answers
2 Sherry is produced in southern Spain.
3 The Rioja region is north-east of Madrid.
4 Bordeaux is produced in the south-west of France .
5 Beaujolais comes from the east of France.
6 The Burgundy wine region is in eastern France.
7 Champagne is produced east of Paris.
8 Riesling comes from western Germany.
9 The Chianti region is south of Florence.
10 Frascati is produced south-east of Rome.

6 **Across**
2 wine list   4 corked   5 Bordeaux
7 Italy   8 Champagne   9 dry

Down
1 full-bodied   3 smooth   6 label
10 room

Unit 12

1
2 GUEST: Could I have a glass of red wine?
 STAFF: Certainly. I'll bring you one.
3 GUEST: Could I/we have some cheese?
 STAFF: Of course. I'll get you some.
4 GUEST: Could we have some menus, please?
 STAFF: Yes. I'll get you some.
5 GUEST: Could I/we have a map of the city?
 STAFF: Yes. I'll just get you one.
6 GUEST: Could I/we have some fresh towels, please?
 STAFF: Certainly. I'll send some up.
7 GUEST: Could we have a table for two?
 STAFF: One moment. I'll see if there's one free.
8 GUEST: Could I/we have some more water, please?
 STAFF: I'll get you some.

2
2 I'll get some.   3 I'll get another.
4 I'll get some.   5 I'll get some.
6 I'll get another.   7 I'll get some more.
8 I'll get one.   9 I'll get some more.
10 I'll get one.

3 2 j 3 g 4 h 5 a 6 f
7 c 8 d 9 i 10 b

4 2 Answer 3 Apologize 4 polite
5 friendly 6 name 7 special
8 patient 9 helpful 10 waiting
11 Smile

5
```
X R I X T O E L E X S A
L I X S C N X M R H N X
X K A X I Z I E X O L K
G O S W A T E R I M X B
T R A E X U N T X E F E
X A L U G G A G E W O X
E X T I X M I N C O X P
N J X L R O X K A R E X
X A D O U N O U X K S S
D X F B R E A D L X A T
O N X M Y A I X O G E
I C E T H X M A Y T X B
```

Unit 13

1 2 g 3 f 4 e 5 d 6 a 7 c

2 2 It consists of fruit juice, croissant or bread, jam, butter, and coffee.
3 It contains lobster, prawns, scallops, and mussels.
4 It consists of tequila, triple sec, lime and lemon juice, and ice.
5 It's made from bread strips, raspberries, and sugar.
6 It contains aubergines, tomatoes, onions, broccoli, and mushrooms.
7 They're made from eggs, milk, and flour.
8 It consists of green salad, tuna, olives, and tomatoes.
9 It's made from olive oil, wine vinegar, and mustard.
10 It consists of pasta, chilli, tomatoes, garlic, basil, and pine nuts.

3 2 Each slice is cut into three or four pieces.
3 Some of the bread strips are put around a pudding bowl.
4 The raspberries are stewed in the sugar for a few minutes.
5 The fruit and some of the juice are added to the pudding bowl.
6 The fruit is covered with more bread strips.
7 The remaining juice is poured over.
8 A weight is put on top of the bowl and it is placed in the refrigerator.

4 2 Put a knife and fork in the plate position.
3 Fold a napkin and place it on a side plate.
4 Bring a dessert spoon and fork with the dessert menu.
5 Place a wine glass above the soup spoon position.
6 Put the salt and pepper in the centre of the table.
7 Place a flower arrangement and a candle by the salt and pepper.

5 1 scallops 2 fish fork 3 lobster
4 hollandaise 5 smoked 6 salmon
7 fish knife 8 king prawn 9 mornay

missing word: chardonnay

Unit 14

1 2 f 3 c 4 a 5 e
6 g 7 h 8 b

2 2 a 3 b 4 d 5 c 6 a
7 c 8 b 9 d 10 a

3 b 10 c 4 d 1 e 7 f 5
g 2 h 9 i 6 j 8

4 2 opened 3 took 4 arrived
5 spoke 6 looked into 7 smiled
8 left 9 gave 10 reserved
11 met 12 shook

5 2 arrived 3 was not 4 gave
5 did not want 6 booked 7 made
8 waited 9 took 10 was
11 complained 12 spoke

6 Across
4 tasteless 6 filthy 7 tough
11 vinegary 12 salty 13 watery
14 rude

Down
1 overcooked 2 dusty 3 stringy
5 flat 8 noisy 9 broken
10 stale

Unit 15

1 3 the reception manager
4 the hotel manager
5 She is responsible for
6 receptionists, reservations, porters
7 the housekeeper
8 She is responsible to
9 She is responsible for
10 the cleaners, attendants
11 the head chef
12 He is responsible for
13 They are responsible to
14 chef, pastry, commis, porters

2 2 h 3 f 4 a 5 j
6 d 7 i 8 b 9 l
10 e 11 g 12 k

3 2 These 3 That 4 Those
5 These 6 that 7 that
8 these/those 9 This 10 those

4 2 b 3 c 4 c 5 c 6 a
7 b 8 d 9 b 10 a

5
```
R S T O C K P O T N O X
E X S A U C E P A N X K
F I H X R T X P M O I D
R S O L X T G E N X B I
I X B L E N D E R D A S
G R X K I X V E L X O H
E X A Y X O R V X M E W
R X B C X Q U I X A H A
A F B A K I N G T I N S
T X A M O X K I L X C H
O W H X O L X S T O X E
R X J F X T O A S T E R
```

Unit 16

1 2 a 3 d 4 a 5 b 6 c
7 b 8 d 9 b 10 a

2 2 e 3 d 4 f 5 c 6 a

3 5, 6, 4, 1, 3

4 2 Strip 3 Put 4 Take
5 Make 6 Clean and dust 7 Clean
8 Empty 9 Replace 10 Check

5 2 You *mustn't* overcook the vegetables.
3 Guests *don't have to* check out until 12 noon.
4 Akiko *doesn't have to* work on Thursdays. It's her day off.
5 Staff *mustn't* wash their hands in the food preparation sinks.
6 Room attendants *don't have to* change the towels every day.
7 Staff *mustn't* smoke in the kitchen.
8 Staff *mustn't* be rude to customers.
9 The kitchen porters *don't have to* scrape the new potatoes.
10 Reception staff *mustn't* keep guests waiting.

6 2 have to 3 must 4 have to
5 have to 6 must 7 have to
8 have to 9 have to 10 must

7 1 hand basin 2 rolling pin 3 balloon whisk
4 utensils 5 toiletries 6 colander
7 towels 8 rubbish

missing word: spotless

Unit 17

1 2 h 3 e 4 f 5 b
6 c 7 d 8 a

2 2 needs 3 needs to 4 needs
5 needs to 6 need 7 needs to
8 needs to 9 needs 10 need

3 2 The bed needs making.
3 The underwear needs washing.
4 The dinner jacket needs repairing.
5 The phone needs answering.
6 The minibar needs refilling.
7 The bathroom floor needs cleaning.
8 The towels need changing.
9 The bin needs emptying.
10 The dress needs ironing/pressing.

4 2 It closes at 5 p.m.
3 There's an exchange bureau on the ground floor.
4 There's a travel agency next door to the hotel.
5 I'll send housekeeping up to your room.
6 Ask the doorman about the theatre-booking service.
7 I'll call one immediately.
8 I'll order one straightaway.

5 Across
4 garlic bread 6 soft drink 8 ice cream
10 coffee 11 tea 12 pastry
13 fruit juice

Down
1 french fries 2 pizza 3 beef burger
5 sandwich 7 omelette 9 soup

Unit 18

1 2 catch 3 say 4 speak up
5 hear 6 have 7 spell
8 repeat 9 speak 10 say

2 d c n e l i j a h m f o b g

3 1 Bravo 2 Papa 3 Delta
4 Tango 5 Echo 6 India
7 Golf 8 Juliet 9 Mike
10 November 11 Sierra 12 Foxtrot
13 Alpha 14 Hotel 15 Romeo

4 2 Did Mrs Brett leave a contact number?
Yes, she did.
3 Did Mrs Brett reserve a single room?
No, she didn't.
4 Did the Ronaldos order breakfast for two?
Yes, they did.

5 Did they book a table for 12.30?
   No, they didn't.
6 Did Valerie offer a discount?
   Yes, she did.

5 2 He didn't confirm his reservation in writing.
3 Reception didn't give room 501 the message.
4 Room 222 didn't pay their bill last night.
5 The hotel didn't include breakfast in the special offer.
6 She didn't speak to the duty manager.
7 The head chef didn't make all the main courses and desserts.
8 He didn't reserve a parking space with his booking.

6 2 €200   3 €280   4 €800   5 €450
6 €260   7 €80   8 €330

7
```
B A T T E R Y H X S B X N
X I M X R A N A W X U S U
A X D R X I P N X U R Y M
V I U X Y E X D A X E T B
X B M E X T A S X I C E E
Y O K X R X P E S M H R R
I N T E R N A T I O N A L
C A L L V X Y U P N B G X
X F R X H O P Y R I X G E
B X J L S X H F A L D D X
W H E X H L O X T E D X O
D I A L L I N G T O N E L
X P R A X T E C C X I A N
```

Unit 19

1 1 knee   2 heavy, back
3 cupboard   4 cut, finger
5 fire exit, fire alarm   6 tripped, foot
7 shock, toaster

2 b 4   c 1   d 6   e 5   f 7   g 3

3 2 clear   3 early   4 fast
5 fresh   6 well   7 hard
8 immediately   9 late   10 patiently
11 polite   12 quickly   13 quiet
14 regularly   15 serious   16 slowly

4 2 immediately   3 fresh   4 hard
5 good   6 fast   7 politely
8 patient   9 carefully   10 regularly

5 2 He cooks well.
3 She drives carefully.
4 He works slowly.
5 We regularly have a test drill.
6 He talked seriously about health and safety.
7 Reception staff always answer guests politely.
8 The cashier asked the man to pay immediately.

6 1 fire axe   2 fire exit   3 fire alarm
4 extinguisher   5 fire blanket   6 fire brigade
7 test drill   8 fire doors   9 sand bucket
10 water sprinkler

missing word: first aider

Unit 20

1 2 The conference suite and roof garden.
3 It's on the ground floor.
4 It's on the top floor.
5 They're on the ground floor.
6 The swimming pool and fitness centre.
7 They're on floors one to five.
8 It's in the basement.

2 2 Turn   3 on   4 across
5 through   6 Turn   7 down
8 on   9 opposite   10 Take
11 come out of   12 turn   13 on
14 along   15 at the end   16 past

3 2 hangers   3 shelf
4 pillows   5 drawers
6 light bulbs   7 welcome folder
8 trouser press   9 shaver point

4 2 light bulbs   3 shelf
4 drawers   5 folder
6 minibar   7 air-conditioning
8 mirror   9 bedspread
10 curtains

5 Across
3 ground floor   4 heating
5 wardrobe   8 mattress
10 basement   11 lift

Down
1 corridors   2 lobby
6 bulbs   7 carpet
9 stairs

Unit 21

1 2 outside   3 bus station
4 underground   5 railway station
6 cinema   7 theatres
8 museums   9 gallery

2 2 by boat   3 by plane/air
4 by train   5 by bus
6 by car   7 on foot
8 by bike

3 2 outside   3 on, off   4 straight on
5 towards   6 up   7 across
8 on

4 Model answers
2 Take the White line three stops south to H. Change onto the Green line and go one stop west.
3 Take the Red line one stop east to D. Change onto the White line and go two stops south.
4 Take the Black line one stop south to C. Change onto the Red line and go one stop east to D. Change onto the White line and go one stop north.
5 Take the Green line one stop west to G. Change onto the Black line and go three stops north.

5 Answers depend on town or city.

6
```
K X A B O N D S T R E E T X
N I R V X S M I U T R X V
I N X I G O T X E W Q U T O
G B I N R X S S A T U M O X
H P I C C A D I L L Y A R F
T K I X C I R C U S D R O
S L A S X O R A B M X B O R
B X Y I T I X Y O L P L X D
R A M C X O B A K E R A X C
I X I P P S T R E E T A X I
D V X R O T X A T R X R E R
G G R E E N P A R K A C C
E M A X D O W X L A R H U
C A N A R Y W H A R F X U S
```

Unit 22

1 A fax, email, photocopier, multi-line phones, broadband, video conferencing
B room service, babysitting, pay-per-view films, car hire, swimming pool, laundry

2 2 f   3 d   4 e   5 h   6 b   7 a   8 g

3 2 TV/monitor   3 screen
4 photocopier   5 printer
6 digital projector   7 microphone
8 laptop

4 2 a   3 d   4 g   5 e   6 b   7 h   8 f

5 2 planning   3 conference   4 require
5 single   6 delegates   7 advise
8 conference

6 1 projector   2 photocopier
3 World Wide Web   4 emails
5 broadband   6 printer
7 video conference   8 Internet
9 business   10 website

missing word: PowerPoint

Unit 23

1 b 8   c 1   d 7   e 5   f 3   g 6   h 4

2 2 have, finished   3 has worked
4 have lived   5 hasn't checked in
6 Has, seen   7 hasn't paid
8 has, fallen down   9 haven't given
10 has, cut

3 2 Have you eaten   3 gave
4 cut   5 burnt
6 has fallen   7 Have you called
8 called   9 fell
10 haven't seen

4 2 e   3 a   4 d   5 h   6 g   7 f   8 c

5 2 h   3 a   4 f   5 i
6 b   7 g   8 d   9 c

6 Across
2 a cold   4 flu   6 nurse
7 toothache   8 headache   10 doctor
11 faint

Down
1 burn   3 diarrhoea   5 asthma
9 dentist

Unit 24

1 2 b   3 a   4 b   5 c   6 b   7 a   8 c

2 2 porter   3 service engineer
4 housekeeper   5 room attendant
6 service engineer   7 room attendant
8 maintenance man   9 room attendant

3 2 The luggage should have been taken up.
3 The message should have been passed on.
4 The shirts should have been sent back.
5 The shower should have been fixed.
6 The toiletries should have been replaced.
7 The TV should have been repaired.
8 He should have been given a non-smoking room.

4 2 e 3 h 4 d 5 g 6 c 7 a 8 f

5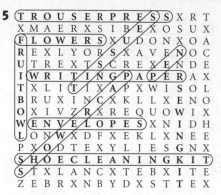

```
T R O U S E R P R E S S S X R T
X M A E R X S I B E X O S U X
F L O W E R S X U D O N X O A
R E X L Y O R S X A V E N O C
U T R E X T S C R E X E N D E
I T W R I T I N G P A P E R A X
T X L I T I X A P X W I S O L
B R U X I N C X K L L X E N O
O X I V Z R X R E Q U O W I X
W E N V E L O P E S X N I D H
L O N W X D F X E K L X N E E
P X O D T E X Y L J E S G N X
S H O E C L E A N I N G K I T
S T X L A N C X T E B X I T E
Z E B R X N B Y D X S T T E X
```

Unit 25

1 2 Credit card   3 Debit card
4 Visa, Mastercard   5 cash
6 Traveller's cheques   7 company
8 receipt   9 VAT
10 vouchers

2 2 is leaving, pays
3 pay
4 leaves
5 is preparing, is helping
6 is leaving, check out
7 signs, gives
8 is serving, serve

3 a 2 her 3 him 4 him 5 it 6 her
b 7 them 8 it 9 it 10 them
c 11 us 12 it 13 us 14 us

4 2 c Australia   3 f China
4 b The UK   5 h Thailand
6 d Russia   7 g India
8 a Japan   9 i Mexico

5 2 k 3 e 4 i 5 c 6 g
7 d 8 j 9 b 10 h 11 f

6 1 invoice   2 total   3 included
4 receipt   5 change   6 service
7 extras   8 itemized

missing word: vouchers

Unit 26

1 2 Restaurant on 09/09 3 Breakfast on 10/9
4 Minibar on 10/09 5 Laundry on 11/09
6 Telephone on 11/09 7 Restaurant on 11/09

2 479.00

3 2 much   3 ✔
4 many/a lot of   5 much/a lot of
6 a lot of   7 ✔
8 much/a lot of   9 a lot of
10 many/a lot of   11 many/a lot of
12 much/a lot of

---

4 1 CASHIER: Certainly, madam.
I'll just print it out for you.
How would you like to pay?
WOMAN: By Visa.
CASHIER: Visa is fine, madam. Here we are.
Three nights, accommodation
with breakfast.
WOMAN: Right. And the extras?
CASHIER: The extras are for the car park,
minibar, and room service.
WOMAN: But I didn't use room service.
CASHIER: Actually madam, the room service
was for dry cleaning and pressing
on Tuesday.
WOMAN: Oh, yes. I forgot. That's right then.

2 WAITER: Straightaway, sir. Here it is.
MAN: Do you take Mastercard?
WAITER: Yes. Mastercard is fine, sir.
MAN: Is service included in the bill?
WAITER: No sir, it isn't included.
MAN: Please add twenty euros to my
Mastercard payment.
WAITER: Twenty euros. Thank you very
much, sir. Just sign here.
MAN: OK. Thank you.
It was a very good meal.

5 Across
4 Fidelio   6 appear
7 checking out   9 guest list
11 items   12 screen
Down
1 departures   2 invoice
3 charges   5 issue
8 click   10 easy

Unit 27

1 2 i 3 j 4 a 5 g 6 d
7 b 8 e 9 h 10 f

2 Curriculum vitae

Surname	Mansky
First name	Ulrika
Address	Mozartstrasse 18, Düsseldorf, Germany 10938
Mobile number	+ 49 7631 24 38 65
Email address	umansky@wanadoo.com
Date of birth	3 April 1986
Education	High School in Düsseldorf Hotel receptionist training in Central College
Qualifications	2004 International Baccalaureate 2004–2005 Diploma in Hotel Reception skills
Work experience	3 years' summer work as receptionist and waitress at Mozarts Hotel
Skills	Excellent word processing, Fidelio-trained, spoken and written English at intermediate level
Personal qualities	Friendly and hard-working. I like responsibility.
References	Frau Margrit Becker, Mozarts Hotel, Mozartstrasse, Düsseldorf

---

3 2 Yours faithfully   3 Dear Mr Pons
4 Yours sincerely   5 Dear Mrs Pons
6 Dear Ms Pons   7 Dear Sir/Madam
8 Would you please send confirmation of
your reservation in writing?
9 With reference to your advertisement in the …
10 I would like to apply for …

4 2 learnt a lot   3 new challenges
4 new menus   5 hardworking professional
6 responsibility   7 travel and other countries
8 use   9 improve
10 driving licence

5
```
R E S P O N S I B I L I T Y
E X M H A R D W O R K I N G
F R A X O L X O L Y M O X S
E A X S L X T O L X I E R O
R Y T I X C W U X T M V A C
E X X O L G X E A B U X S I
N S X U S X O C F A J Z X A
C E X P E R I E N C E X Y B
E A T T X F R I E N D L Y L
D R I V I N G L I C E N C E
X I N L X H A E F E X L T O
N X A R U O G H X N V O U X
P U X O R G A N I Z E D X Y
Q U I K X C H A L L E N G E
```

Unit 28

1
Good interview techniques	How NOT to be
smile	look unhappy
relaxed	tense
positive attitude	negative attitude
speak clearly	speak quietly
smart	badly dressed
confident	nervous
well-prepared	unprepared
well-informed	not well-informed
make eye contact	avoid eye contact

2 2 'm going to have   3 'm going to look for
4 are visiting   5 return
6 'm going to have to   7 'll go
8 'll check   9 'll find
10 'm going to look for 11 are, doing
12 Are, coming   13 'll send

3 2 moved   3 course   4 study
5 taught   6 useful   7 taking
8 dealing   9 stayed   10 leave
11 skills   12 push   13 found
14 joining   15 hotel chain   16 opportunities
17 staff   18 all over   19 spend
20 improve

4 2 in Switzerland   3 aunt Vivienne's brother
4 Charles and Peter   5 cousins
6 nephews and niece

5 1 career   2 candidate   3 shortlist
4 TV series   5 experience   6 teamworker
7 hotel chain   8 interview   9 certificate

missing word: enthusiastic